# The Two Lefts:
# Chávez, Venezuela, and Contemporary Left-Wing Politics

## Teodoro Petkoff

translated by Daniel Petkoff
edited by Matthew Clark

Published by Lulu.com

ISBN  978-1-84753-618-1

**Contents**                                                    **Page**

## Acronyms of political parties and organizations

| | |
|---|---|
| AD [Venezuela] | *Acción Democratica* |
| ALBA | *Alternativa Bolívariana para nuestra América* |
| ALCA | *Área de Libre Comercio de las Américas* |
| AMLO [Mexico] | *Andrés Manuel López Obrador* |
| CD [Venezuela] | *Coordinación Democrática* |
| CNE [Venezuela] | *Consejo Nacional Electoral* (National Electoral Council) |
| Copei [Venezuela] | *Partido Social Cristiano de Venezuela* |
| FAN [Venezuela] | *Fuerza Armada Nacional* (National Armed Forces) |
| FIM [Venezuela] | *Frente Institucional Militar* |
| FLN [Algeria] | *Front de Libération Nationale* |
| FMLN [Salvador] | *Frente Farabundo Martí para la Liberación Nacional* |
| FSLN [Nicaragua] | *Frente Sandistina Liberación de Nicaragua* |
| MAS [Bolivia, Venezuela] | *Movimiento al Socialismo* |
| MIR [Chile, Venezuela] | *Movimiento de Izquierda Revolucionaria* |
| MNR [Bolivia] | *Movimiento Nacionalista Revolucionario* |
| NPE | *Nueva Política Económica* (New Political Economy) |
| OEA | *Organización de Estados Américanos* |
| OMC | *Organización Mundial del Comercio* (World Trade Organization) |
| PCV [Venezuela] | *Partido Comunista Venezolano* |
| PDVSA [Venezuela] | *Petroléos de Venezuela Sociedad Anónima* |
| PLD [Dominican Republic] | *Partido de la Liberación Dominicano* |
| PMDB [Brazil] | *Partido del Movimiento Democrático Brasileño* |
| PPP [Guyana] | *Partido Popular Progresista* |
| PRD [Mexico, Panama] | *Partido de la Revolución Democrática* |
| PSDB [Brazil] | *Partido de la Social Democracia Brasilera* |
| PT [Brazil] | *Partido dos Trabalhadores* |
| PT [Venezuela] | *Partido de los Trabajadores* |
| RR | *Referéndo Revocatorio* (Recall Referendum) |
| SIP | *Sociedad Interamericana de Prensa* (Inter- American Press Association) |

## Editor's preface

This volume comprises a collection of essays written between 2002 and 2004 by Teodoro Petkoff, who during the last four decades has been one of Venezuela's most prominent politicians and political thinkers. He is still very active politically; in 2006 he joined the opposition campaign, briefly as the front-runner, in the presidential race against Hugo Chávez. Since 2000, he has been the editor of *Tal Cual*, one of the most widely read newspapers in Venezuela. First published in Spanish as *Dos Izquierdas* (Caracas: Alfadil, 2005), this book has been translated with a view to introducing Petkoff's comment and analysis to the English-speaking world, as none of his previous publications has been translated into English. While an attempt has been made to convey the sense of the original Spanish as accurately as possible, the text has been extensively rewritten in order to render the prose into what is hopefully more readable English. Several footnotes have been added to explain references that may be familiar to Venezuelans but which may be less so to English readers.

Matthew Clark
Hove, England, May 2007

**Prologue**

A simple survey of the political map of our continent during the first five years of the twenty-first century demonstrates an inarguable fact: Latin America has shifted politically towards the left.

In the words of Joaquín Villalobos: "In the entire continent, the left is either in government, or at least constitutes half of the power, or it is fighting its own orthodoxy and immaturity, but nowhere is it weak".[1]

However, this does not mean that Cuba, Chile, Brazil, Uruguay, Argentina, the Dominican Republic, Venezuela, Ecuador or Mexico all constitute an immovable block of Latin American "socialist" nations. But among the implications of this phenomenon is that the debate of ideas in the region—a debate that not more than a decade ago seemed to have been reduced to the small group of topics being discussed by what is now the quite barren "consensus of Washington"—now needs to deal with the additional problems raised by the "viability" of a democracy of the Latin American left. This is all taking place in a continent that is no longer under the authoritarian "protection" of the American Department of State, but where extreme poverty has produced a population that is politically more impatient than it was in the 1950s and 1960s.

Consider the political parties in the region: besides Lula Da Silva's PT (*Partido de los Trabajadores*) and, of course, the unique party represented by Fidel Castro himself, there is the Mexican PRD (*Partido de la Revolución Democrática*), there are Chilean socialists around President Lagos, the coalition of left-wing parties that support Hugo Chávez in Venezuela, the FMLN (*Frente Farabundo Martí para la Liberación Nacional*) of Schafick Handal in El Salvador, the *Frente Amplio* ("Extended Front") of the Uruguayan president Tabaré Vázquez, Evo Morales' MAS (*Movimiento al Socialismo*), the so-called *Polo Democrático* (Democratic Pole) in Colombia, Juan Bosch's and Leonel Fernández's PLD (*Partido de la Liberación Dominicano*) in the Dominican Republic, Martin Torrijos' PRD (*Partido de la Revolución Democrática*) in Panama—the list is striking, isn't it?; and notice the frequent inclusion of the term "democratic" in the names of the parties. It seems obvious that these parties do not unanimously embody an equal and shared vision of the public policies which could best confront the task of removing poverty from their countries, nor do they share the same vision of the role of the state, the division of powers, civil society, periodic elections, freedom of expression and the rights of minorities, just to mention a few of the topics of politically liberal thought that would not have not caused a left-winger in the region to lose any sleep in the proverbial 1960s.

Without doubt, what is happening now is not a new or unprecedented debate: what else was the tragic unfolding of the dilemma between dogmatism and a sense of reality that was embodied in the opposition between the Cuban Revolution and the "experiment" led by Allende? Consider the tolerant mood of the overthrown president towards Augusto Pinochet: Allende's experiment at

---

[1] Joaquín Villalobos, "Bush y las izquierdas latinoamericanas", *El Diario de Hoy*, San Salvador, 13/4/2005.

least sought support in a pluralist tradition and conformed to the provisions of a democratic constitution.

At that time, the debate was won by the "heavyweights". However, the conditions in which we are presently holding this debate *are* unprecedented: it is less than fifteen years since the fall of the Berlin wall and the collapse of the Soviet Union, and we are in a situation where the United States cannot make further inroads into the life of our continent, even should they wish to. Any kind of military intrusion would have unpredictable consequences for the USA, even if they were to be temporarily victorious.

In the arena of Latin-American left-wing politics, two opposing types of profile are being defined. One of these profiles is the kind of left wing that could be called "Bourbon",[2] as so felicitously described by Petkoff: this is a kind of extremely blind conservatism that has no future and which has values with no real content. A large part of the left that Chávez has gathered around himself belongs to that camp. The same has been done by Handal's FMLN and Evo Morales' MAS; their tutelary figure is Fidel Castro, and in that sense they are "Bourbon", in other words reactionary.

The other camp is the one that includes Tabaré Vázquez, Ricardo Lagos or Lula Da Silva: they have no essential tutelary figures, nor fixed, fundamentalist or hypocritical dogmas to which they are irrevocably wedded. They have, however, the formidable and urgent challenge of successfully advancing the fight against poverty and exclusion, but without killing democracy.

Teodoro Petkoff has been a pioneer of the democratic camp within this debate, ever since he first opened fire almost forty years ago with what has become an unavoidable classic of Latin American political thought, *Checoslovaquia: El Socialismo como problema (Czechoslovakia: Socialism as a problem)*.

As chief editor of the daily newspaper *Tal Cual*, which he has been for the last five years, and through his weekly television program, Teodoro has day by day explained the currently polarized political situation in Venezuela. The scope of his extensive political experience, his undoubted intellectual integrity, his natural ability to clarify controversy, and his commitment to social justice and democracy pervade his penetrating analysis. His editorials have become a beacon of the genuinely democratic opposition to Chávez's government.

*The Two Lefts* comprises a significant collection of essays written by Teodoro in recent times. Some have been published previously, either in the daily newspaper *Tal Cual*, or in other Latin American publications, appearing in the magazines *Cambio* and *Diner's* (from Colombia), in the prestigious *Nueva Sociedad*, and as prologues for the books *América y Fidel Castro*, by Américo Martín (Caracas: Panapo, 2001) and *Hugo Chávez sin uniforme* (Caracas:

---

[2] Petkoff uses the term "Bourbon" to designate what in Britain used to be called "red" communists. Historically, "Bourbon" refers to a member of the family which long held the thrones of France and Naples, and until 1930, that of Spain. In the USA in the late nineteenth century, the term "Bourbon" was also occasionally used to refer to an "unteachable Democrat", hence the quip: "one who learns nothing and forgets nothing".

Debate, 2005), the latter being a political biography recently published in Caracas by Cristina Marcano and Alberto Barrera Tyzka.

Some of these essays tackle and deeply explore a necessary characterization of the two Latin-American political "lefts". The "physiology" of Fidel's cult and the nature of Chávismo—which is an exemplary manifestation of the "Bourbon" left—are contrasted with the shades and particularities of the other kind of "left", which has been rejected by some as being merely "pragmatic" but which has nevertheless been adopted by Lula, Lagos and Tabaré Vázquez, a project that Teodoro occasionally describes as "avant-garde reformism".

In this regard, in one of his editorials in which he celebrated the assumption of power by Tabaré Vázquez in Uruguay, Petkoff recently wrote:

> Although the romantic sex-appeal and the shots of adrenalin induced by the Castro-Chávez version of the "left" finds an echo in some of the countries where the left seems to be ready to accede to power (Nicaragua, El Salvador, Bolivia), concrete experiences of it are not at all inspiring: on one hand, consider Cuba, which is a ruined and totalitarian country; and on the other hand, consider the confusing "Bolívarian Revolution"[3]…"In any case" he concluded, "Latin America is opening a new chapter in its history, its destiny no longer determined by the contingencies of the Cold War; it is taking account of its own circumstances and of its long and tortuous evolution.

These words about the Latin American left coherently set out Petkoff's vision of the global situation, which—whether or not we want it—has been affected by imperialist policy after the traumatic terrorist attacks on New York on 9/11/2001. These observations are complemented with a few impressions of a recent trip to China and a reflection on Chávez and Islam.

"What does the *catire*[4] Petkoff say; how do you see the problem Teodoro"? These are usually Venezuelans' favourite questions, whether they are "*Chávistas*" or "*escuálidos*".[5] The questions are generally raised in order to ignite a conversation about our political crisis, which is as equally as distressing as it is difficult to get a grip on.

This volume also includes previously unpublished essays, deliberately conceived to be integrated into this anthology. One of them provides a meticulous and penetrating analysis of the role fulfilled by the media within the political Venezuelan crisis. Another presents a lucid and balanced assessment of

---

[3] This is a reference to Chávez's frequent invocation of the Venezuelan hero, Simón Bolívar (Simón José Antonio de la Santísima Trinidad Bolívar Palacios y Blanco, 1783–1830), South America's most revered revolutionary. Born in Caracas, Bolívar—also referred to as *El Libertador* (the "Liberator")—led the fight for independence from the Spanish in the countries that are now named Bolivia, Colombia, Ecuador, Panama, Peru and Venezuela. Chávez employs the well-known image of Bolívar as a symbol of his own "revolution".

[4] *Catire* means "fair-skinned" or "blond", and is a nickname of Teodoro Petkoff, deriving from his childhood, when his was one of the only white families in a black village.

[5] *Escuálidos* means the "squalid" ones, and is a term frequently used these days to refer to the political opposition.

the Venezuelan opposition in the situation that emerged after the referendum on the 15th of August 2004.

Recommending Petkoff's brilliant essays is really almost redundant at this stage, but, as a reader, I would not want to finish without also calling attention to the brilliant Introduction of this book ("Gabo: by way of an Introduction"), which is an article that reflects on the friendship that faithfully unites Teodoro Petkoff with Gabriel García Márquez—who is incontrovertibly the living icon of the Bourbon left—and on Petkoff's own path as one of the most influential politicians and intellectuals in public life during the last half a century in Venezuela.

Ibsen Martínez<br>Caracas, April 2005

**Gabo**[6]
(By way of an Introduction)


Gabo has told the episode of Pérez Jiménez's[7] fall a thousand and one times. It was the year 1958, and Gabo was in Caracas, working as a reporter for the magazine *Momento*. But it was not then that we met, even though Gabo was already among us. He was happy, without I.D., and living more or less in anonymity; and I was a communist student, even more anonymous, coming from a clandestine struggle against a dictatorship, and just beginning what would become a long career in public life. It was many years later that I heard about Gabo for the first time. I was a prisoner in the San Carlos barracks, an old colonial fortress converted into a military prison, and around 1966 I came across a newspaper article—which I read because in prison one reads even the classified ads—that was about a novel by a Colombian writer, by whom I hadn't yet read anything. Gabo, who was then living in Mexico, had just produced a novel entitled *Cien añios de soledad (One Hundred Years of Solitude)*. It caught my attention, because around that time I had been cultivating a keenness for writing, which fortunately for the history of Venezuelan literature culminated in just seven short stories and a novel, the latter being so bad that I destroyed it, consigning it to the flames of a bonfire of self-criticism. Everything that had to do with literature aroused my curiosity.

A few months later, in 1967, two memorable events happened to me: I escaped from the San Carlos barracks for the second time and I read *One Hundred Years of Solitude,* in that order. It has to be said that this last event dazzled me, as it did everybody else. At that time I probably thought I would have liked to meet the author, but also I probably said to myself that there weren't any reasons for such a thing to happen, since, I imagined, we circled in very different orbits: he was already "García Márquez", and I, well, I was a nobody. I was wrong. A short while later I found out that we were inhabiting the same world, the very stormy, tormented, contradictory and colourful world of the Latin American left. Also, we were then living in the small circle of those on the left who had started asking ourselves if what we wanted for our countries was similar to what existed in the Soviet Union and its eastern block, because "real socialism" was already generating many doubts. As absurd and strange as it may sound, it was Gabo who contacted me, and not the other way around, as might have been expected. This was owing to reasons imposed by what might be called a "law of gravity". As a consequence of developments in Venezuelan political affairs, somehow Gabo had been following me with some distant attention. Towards the end of 1969 or maybe the first part of the following year, I had started circulating an essay, *Checoeslovaquia: El socialismo como problema (Czechoslovakia: Socialism as a Problem).* Just the title was a manifesto in itself. I mention this briefly, without any major digressions, simply because the essay addressed the

---

[6] The nickname of the author Gabriel García Márquez.

[7] President (and dictator) of Venezuela from 1952 to 1958.

thorny issue that was tackled by a Venezuelan communist militant the following year, after troops of the Soviet Union had invaded Czechoslovakia. It suffices to say that Leonid Brezhnev, who by then was the General Secretary of the Communist Party in the Soviet Union and Prime Minister of his all-powerful country, included my name in his small cast of "enemies of communism" who he condemned in his report to the Party during the twenty-fourth Congress in 1970. I could imagine the Europeans' surprise, asking themselves who the hell was that distant Latin-American man who had the "honour" of having his name recorded alongside two of the most famous Marxist philosophers, the Frenchman Roger Garaudy and the Austrian Ernest Fischer. Also included in that list was the Italian group *Il Manifesto*, who were already known globally, and all branded as "heretics" of the communist movement. But the inclusion of my name wasn't for lack of reasons, for in that essay I had not only condemned the invasion of Czechoslovakia—considering it to be an action symmetrical to the invasion of Santo Domingo by the United States three years earlier—but I also allowed myself to reject the validity the Soviet "model". That was the end of the world!

Anyhow, some time later, after my book entered the public domain, I received a card from the hands of Soledad Mendoza (Plinio Apuleyo's sister),[8] simply signed "Gabo." It contained ten lines written in black ink, in which Gabo mentioned how impressed he was with my book, and announcing that very soon we would be meeting. It is important to pay attention to the following detail. By 1970, the Cuban revolution had already held for a little more than ten years, and Gabo was already an intimate friend of Fidel Castro, who had supported the Soviet invasion of "tiny" Czechoslovakia in one of those proverbial acrobatic manoeuvres dictated by reasons of state. Without a doubt, by the time Gabo wrote to me he must have spent many hours talking about the issue with Fidel, and they must have had some sort of disagreement. However, as on many other occasions, Fidel, privately, could have been in agreement with his friend and was instead trying to explain to him the political reasons why he had to support the USSR, which only a few people in Cuba held in high esteem. At least, this is how Gabo once explained it to me, though to fully understand the events we'll have to wait for him to tell the story in his memoirs. But what is evident is that at that time Gabo had begun to get very disillusioned with the communist world.

Nevertheless, the matter did not end in a mere intellectual gesture. In 1971, the *Movimiento al Socialismo* (MAS) had already been founded, becoming a true *bête noire* for the world's communist movements, and considered by Fidel's followers as a sort of traitor's lair. That was when Gabo made contact with us, during carnival or the holy week of either 1971 or '72. I was spending a few days with my family in a borrowed house in Naiguata, a small village by the coast, when unexpectedly they appeared there (I never knew how they found the place): Miguel Otero Silva[9] and Gabo. At that time, Miguel continued to believe that in the USSR they really were forging "the songs of tomorrow", and for that reason he cordially despised me, but, always a gentleman, he had agreed to put

---

[8] Plinio Apuleyo Mendoza, a well-known Colombian writer (b. 1932).

[9] A Venezuelan author and politician.

us in contact with each other. It was then, while we were sitting around with a few beers and a fish stew, that Gabo said he considered himself an "international" militant of MAS, a political party that we had founded in January of 1971, right after leaving the Communist Party in December of the previous year. It didn't take long for him to demonstrate this. In August of 1972 he won the "Rómulo Gallegos" literary award and proceeded to donate to us the entire amount of the award, which was $22.500, and a lot of money at that time. Such was the sum that we were able to launch a daily newspaper, *Punto.* Though for Gabo this meant a public compromise. He was taking a stand in the world's communist movements that were against the USSR, but mostly against the Cubans. He placed himself to the left of the political spectrum, though he was clearly saying that his idea of socialism had nothing to do with the kind of society that had been erected in its name in the USSR. And somehow, indirectly, he was also speaking to Fidel. I intuitively believe that apart from what Gabo thought—and Fidel knew what Gabo thought—he never resented their friendship. Many years later, during Christmas of 1997, at his house in La Havana, Gabo told me a moving anecdote. A high-ranking group of officials were talking with Fidel and Gabo. He made a few critical observations about the regime and one member of the group inquired what exactly he meant by those remarks. It was Fidel who answered: "What Gabo means to say is that neither he nor I like the revolution that we have made". You could imagine the heavy silence that fell on the group after such a bitter confession had been made.

As the years went by, we saw each other from time to time in different places around the world. I believe I have visited all of his houses: the ones in Barcelona, London, Mexico, Bogotá, Cartagena and La Havana. In all of them there was always the serene presence and good taste of his wife, Mercedes. I don't remember in which one of them he gave me the manuscript of *El otoño del patriarca (The Autumn of the Patriarch)* to read. On one of those occasions we discussed, among other things, the issue of Franco, and suddenly he said, thoughtfully, "What could 'power' be? It's like a small ball that some have in their hands, which they caress constantly". I believe this topic constitutes his great obsession—and therefore a fascination—which brings him close to those men who hold the "little ball". A particular example of his fascination is the Latin-American Colonel Aureliano Buendía.[10] These kinds of people seem to be an object of permanent study for him. Whatever Gabo leaves in his memoirs about his relationship with Fidel Castro, which has lasted for four decades, might constitute one of the most passionate political testimonies of the century.

In 1978 or beginnings of 1979, Gabo told me over the 'phone that he was coming to Caracas. He was coming more or less incognito, as he didn't want to see anybody, and he said he would explain everything after his arrival in the country. Once he had arrived he revealed to me that he was carrying a message from Fidel to Carlos Andres Pérez, and he asked me to put him in touch with the president. This was not difficult at all, because at that time, which was not so long ago, the relationship between the opposition and government in our country was

---

[10] One of the main characters in *One Hundred Years of Solitude.*

still very civilized. The message was about the preparations of the Sandinistas for their first "final offensive"—the one that failed, before a successful second one—and they were thinking of installing a sort of provisional government in Nica territory, for which international recognition would be necessary. They hoped Pérez would be able to do that. There were also talks about material help, and I believe this is where the ties between Carlos Andres Pérez and Nicaragua began, which many years later ended up not with the Sandinistas but with their opponents in power, and unfortunately, with Pérez being sent to jail. At that time, a few hours before leaving, Gabo played another one of his "pranks": because his visit to us had turned out exactly how he had wanted it—and had not produced any unwanted repercussions—he managed to organize an interview with me for the newspaper *El Nacional*, which was not only a literary success but also a political one: Gabo had come to Caracas solely for the purpose of meeting with "his Party".

In 1983, I became the presidential candidate for MAS. It was the first of two symbolic candidatures, which I assumed during a time when there seemed to be an eternal and armour-plated bi-partisanship between AD (*Accion Democratica*) and Copei (*Partido Social Cristiano de Venezuela*). Being among those who fought against the deficiencies and perversions that would eventually culminate in their downfall, we were seen as nothing short of demented. It then occurred to Gabo that he could help us from Colombia. Having ties to the publishing company "La Oveja Negra", he went through the formalities for the Colombian publication of my book *Proceso a la izquierda (Process towards the Left)*. Then he overwhelmed me by presenting the book in an auditorium in Bogotá. I can't really say that the "whole of Colombia" was there, because Gabo himself had already shown me how limited those kinds of hyperbolic statements are. On another occasion, during an event being held in his honour, an enthusiastic admirer exclaimed that "the whole of Colombia was here". Gabo quickly glanced around the room and said: "Yes? Where is Kid Pambele?"[11] And as a matter of fact, that day, the day of the presentation of my book, Pambele was not there, but as Agustin Lara's song goes, "the cream of the intellectuals" and of the politicians was there. But, as for me, who would miss an invitation to one's own Nobel Prize ceremony in Colombia?

The following day, that fabulous party, which was like an event for a patron saint, ended up with lunch at a restaurant in Bogotá. There were only a few of us, not more that eight or ten. But one of them was none other than Belizario Betancur, president of the country to boot. Some time later Gabo told me that the restaurant owner did not cash the check he had given to pay the bill. He framed it and it is now hanging on one of the walls of his place. It was around that time that Gabo wrote, as another form of contribution to "his Party", an article about me that he simply entitled "Teodoro", which was then published in many newspapers around the continent. Curiously, but understandably, it didn't appear in any of the newspapers in my country.

---

[11] Antonio "Kid Pambele" Cervantes, born in 1945 in Bolívar, Colombia, became a welterweight boxer and one of South America's most famous sportsmen.

In relating all of this, I am not trying to foster some sort of religious adulation by the reader, nor because my personal involvement had any major importance, but because through those gestures, Gabo, who is not very keen on making political speeches, nevertheless defined a position, saying, "I think as I act and I act as I think". Having the advantage of knowing Havana's point of view, he was an exceptional witness of the ins and outs of Latin-American left-wing politics. He always saw the political process of national reconciliation in Venezuela at the end of the 60's as "emblematic". It was in the way that we, the communists, understood that armed conflicts were a serious mistake. We developed a line of progressive retreat, which opened up a way towards pacification and the normalization of national political life. How many times did I hear him presenting our case as an example of what he would have liked for his own country, where on many occasions he generously gave his efforts in the cause of pacifism!

As I already said, we haven't seen each other since the Christmas of 1997 in Havana. I do not belong to MAS any longer—I retired from it in mid-1998—and Gabo had already broken ties quietly from us. I understand him: disappointment is the name of the game. On occasions we speak over the 'phone, especially because we now share the same trade, journalism. He continues being the same Gabo as always: now famous, but still happy and without I.D.

Teodoro Petkoff
Caracas, September 22nd, 2002

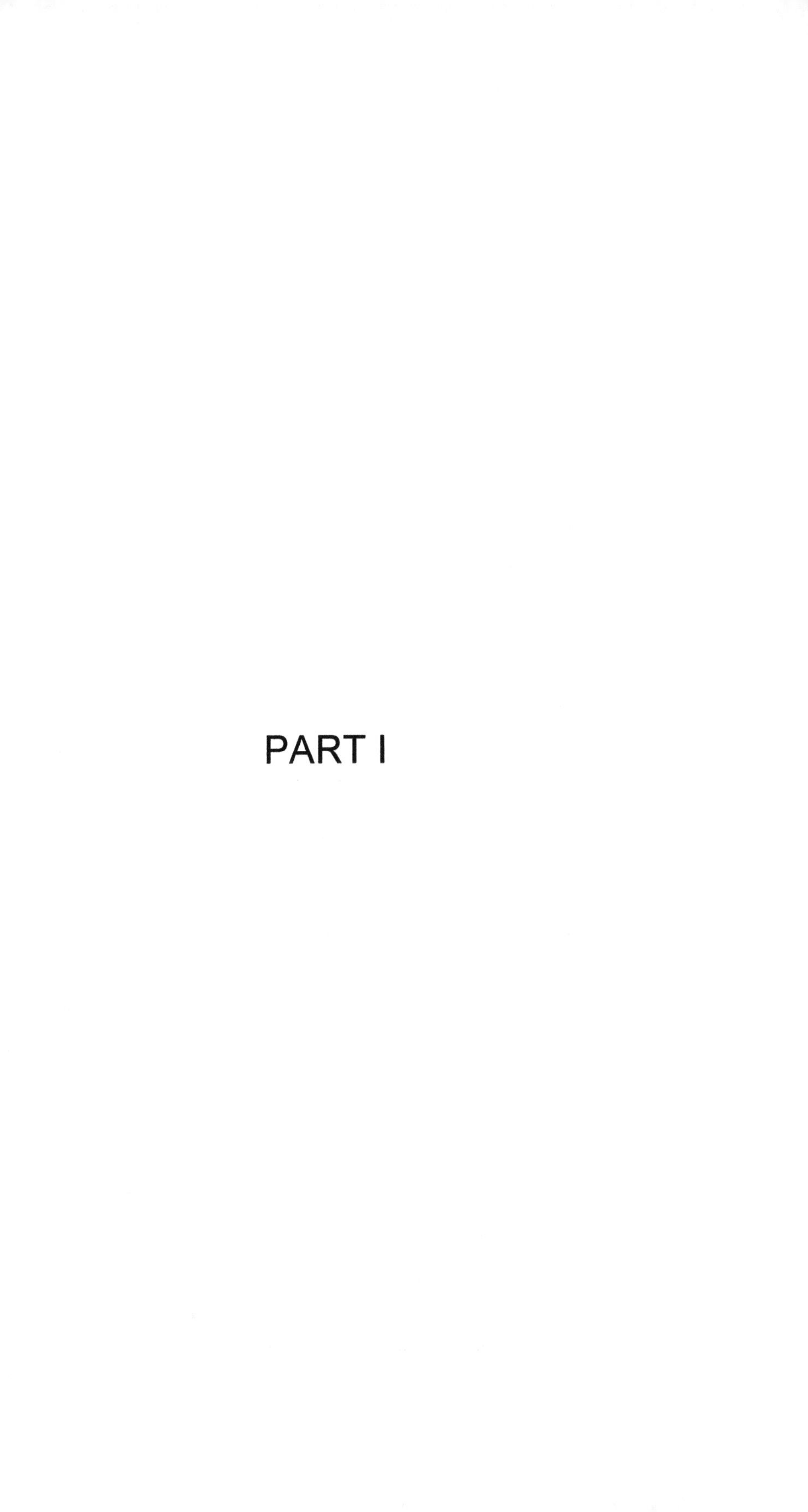

# PART I

**The two lefts**

With Tabare Vasquez's recent assumption of power in Uruguay, a new political milestone has been established, in what might be described as a Copernican-like turn towards the left in the Latin-American continent and the Caribbean. The leaders of all the governments in this region, namely Fidel in Cuba, Tabare in Uruguay, Lula in Brazil, Jagdeo in Guyana, Kirchner in Argentina, Lago in Chile, Chávez in Venezuela, Torrijo in Panama, and Leonel Fernandez in Dominican Republic, already head nine left-wing regimes. If we add to this the related phenomenon that in Nicaragua the Sandinista Movement is shaping up towards a comeback to power, that in El Salvador the FMLN controls the parliament and the majority of the municipalities, and that the Bolivian MAS has become the strongest political power, you could say that we are witnessing a historical tendency, one of profound change in the continent's political temper. We are not witnessing a series of isolated episodes, or disconnected opportunities that arose at various times, such as what happened in Cuba in 1959, in Chile with Allende in 1970, or in Nicaragua with the Sandinista Movement in 1979. The continent's people, its rural and urban masses, who are usually beyond the reach of the traditional political parties and their leaders' sermons, are placing their hopes and expectations on the left side of the political spectrum. Without making comparisons between different societies, or viewing political events from the simple perspective of a Manichaean kind of duality, and also without getting sided-tracked in specific details, it may be seen that decades spent developing military dictatorships and populist and/or neo-liberal democracies has altogether resulted in a legacy of institutional degradation, corruption, contradictory ideas and poor economic growth in some of the most unjust and unequal societies in the world, which are in a condition of permanent social crisis and political instability.

We are, of course, using the term "left" in a generic way, deliberately simplistic and schematic, given that the nuances and differences in all the left-leaning governments we have mentioned are very marked. Later on we will tackle this aspect of the issue.

As paradoxical as it may seem, this is a phenomenon that is inseparable from the collapse of the Soviet empire. With the disintegration of the Soviet empire, together with the disappearance of the logic of the cold war, the movements and progressive political parties of the world—particularly in Latin-America and the Caribbean, which are so far from the hand of God and so close to the United States—no longer stumble along under the ceiling imposed on their aspirations by the implacable determinism of the influence deriving from the "equilibrium of terror" that existed between USSR and the United States. Both superpowers made sure not to allow the emergence, in their respective geopolitical areas, of governments that could be suspected of even remotely or in any way serving the strategy of their archrivals. Moreover, an unspoken rule of their confrontation was to reduce protest against the abuses generated by themselves in "their own" spheres of influence to the level of mere diplomatic formalities. On the one side, the United States did not show any willingness to push the nuclear buttons in the "defence" of either Hungary, Czechoslovakia, Poland or Afghanistan; while on the other side, neither did the USSR make any moves in the "defence" of Guatemala, Santo Domingo, Nicaragua or Chile. The implication was that each superpower had the "right" to prevent—and even destroy if they couldn't prevent it—the adoption of political solutions in countries that were in "their" areas of influence, and which were not coherent with the respective geo-political and geo-strategic paradigms of the two superpowers. This political situation on the world-stage was disturbed by Cuba, which, in 1961, announced that it had become socialist, with a government that had attached itself to the Soviet conclave. This was a consequence of an unexpected process, which took the United States by surprise: it had been a *fait accompli*. The missile crisis in October of 1962 produced an agreement that definitively permitted the permanent establishment of a socialist government, but it also closed off any possibility that the USSR might use Cuban territory for any sort of military purpose. The missile crisis made it apparent—to the extent that the consequences were assumed by the Americans as well as the Soviets—that the spheres of influence on each side were effectively untouchable. Of course, it was also implicit in the political situation that each superpower had the "right" to support and even promote political movements with which they had some affinity on the "other side". However, it was also implicit that the superpowers would disengage themselves from those spheres of potential influence without any remorse at all, should the equilibrium risk being compromised. It was a dynamic world and both superpowers knew it. The crucial point underlying that dynamism was not to exceed the limitations that each of the empires considered inviolable in relation to its own security. The United States Invaded Santo Domingo, favoured the removal of Pinochet (the *Pinochetazo*) in Chile, and armed the opposition in Nicaragua. In comparison, the Soviet Union invaded Hungary, Czechoslovakia and Afghanistan and gave an auspicious start to Jaruzelski's *coup d'état* in Poland. Africa and south-east Asia constituted a sort of "no man's land", where the two big blocks confronted each other vicariously, as this area did not especially affect the balance of power in their respective spheres of influence, whatever might have been the outcome of confrontations in those regions. So, for example, the wars in Korea, Vietnam, Zaire, Angola and Ethiopia did not alter the *status quo* of the world.

All of this changed once the USSR disappeared as a viable political entity. As a consequence, American policy makers subsequently stopped perceiving left-wing governments in Latin America and the Caribbean as threats to their strategic interests. No longer was there a great rival to be afraid of, a fear that had previously been exploited for political purposes. In the United States, we now find much less paranoia among those who make the decisions: the "*Dr. Strangelove* syndrome" has diminished. However, after the illusions of the New World Order vanished in smoke—the "New World Order" being not only the name given to the *Pax Americana*, but also representing a kind of Hegelian and Fukuyama-like "end of history"—the world got complicated again. The USA has scaled up the war on drug trafficking, now reaching into Latin America, and a global war against terrorism has been declared. These global enemies, nevertheless, are not embodied in any great superpower with nuclear fangs. This is the reason why, in the continent of the Americas, there is room for politics and for governments that are not necessarily compliant with Washington; they have not been repressed in the same way as they would have been during that long half-century of the cold war. There is not, at least so far, a new dialectic between global power blocks. In the era of the USSR, the United States would have never invaded Iraq, which was located in the lower belly of what used to be the communist superpower. Now, instead, the USA spreads its troops all over the entire map of the world. The north-American sphere of influence is now global, but without the threat of an atomic disaster there is a lot more room for manoeuvre for those governments that are not aligned with Washington. This explains why left-wing governments in Latin-America and the Caribbean, which only a few years ago could not have been constituted, today coexist with the United States without any major frictions; apart from the specific case of Hugo Chávez, for reasons that we will analyse later on.

At the same time, the left-wing parties that nowadays govern some Latin American countries and the Caribbean do not answer to the stereotypical Manichaeian image that has been coined by the *gringos:* that "left-wing equals communism". Not only has the Soviet Union disappeared, but the world's communist movement has been reduced to the condition of an archaeological exhibit. There have never been major communist parties in Latin America and the Caribbean, but as political limbs of the Soviet "Vatican" these communist parties possessed an undeniable influence; so much so that they could exert blackmail over the entire left-wing movement. For example, they were able to silence any criticism of the USSR and "real socialism". For the Latin American left, the association with the USSR and communism, even if it was full of frictions and plagued by contradictions and misunderstandings, constituted a heavy mortgage from which it was difficult to break free. This was because the opponents of left wing and politicians and spokesmen of the effective powers of the right wing made anti-communism and denouncing the Soviet regime—and in our continental case, the Cuban regime—one of the essential fundamentals of their politics: the enemy of my enemy, if he is not my friend, is also neither my enemy. Furthermore, Latin America, with its long history of American imperialism, and having incurred numerous military interventions—including frictions between the United States and non left-wing governments—drove the Latin American left wing to take an uncritical position against the USSR. So, of course, this was useful for both the national opposition against the left wing as well as for the *gringos.* It was useful to be able to throw everything in the same basket, labelling all left-wing movements "communist". Many of these movements, moreover, responded to the stereotypical and rudimentary anti-communism of their adversaries with an anti-Americanism, if not anti-imperialism, which was equally primitive and rudimentary. But this only produced a vicious circle.

It seems as though the disappearance of the USSR has created the conditions for the complete re-establishment of an ideological and political autonomy for the left wing. The left no longer has to carry the dead weight symbolised by the totalitarian, dictatorial and economically failed model of the USSR. According to the opposition's propaganda—which produced a potent deterrent effect in our countries—this model represented the "mirror" of "progressive ideas"; but the left can no longer be either checked or blackmailed by the communist movement. The relationship between Cuba and Chávez, Bolivia's MAS and the Sandinista movement has some special characteristics. In these cases there is a political and ideological affinity that does not pertain to any other of our left-wing movements. This relationship evidently produces an inhibiting effect similar to that previously produced by the sinister image of the USSR. In the case of Cuba—not only in the left wing but beyond it—their rejection of the stolid American political stance towards the island, which is coupled with a strong Latin-American feeling, has led to a sort of indulgence in a feeling of empathy with the idea of the small David against the giant Goliath; especially as there is also a desire to invoice the giant for felonies perpetrated in what is pejoratively considered to be their own "backyard", or *mare nostrum.*

Now, the concept of "the left" can be confusing. It covers a lot more than it reveals, and if applied indiscriminately could lead to enormous mistakes of understanding.

In the left wing as well as in the right wing we can find many nuances of difference. For example, in the opposing positions of Hitler and Churchill you could find any number of common expressions of conservative thinking; or, for example, between the two positions represented by Stalin and Tony Blair: there are many gradations from the centre towards the left. However, as a consequence of the analysis that has been presented, it could be pointed out that, broadly speaking, there currently exist two left wings in Latin-America, two great currents moreover, in some cases homogeneous but each one of them having a variety of specific nuances. One of the two major currents of the left wing today has as its greatest exponents the governments of Lula, Lagos, Kirchner and Vasquez, and with a lower profile, the governments of Leonel Fernandez in the Dominican Republic, Martin Torrijos in Panama, and Bharret Jagdeo in Guyana. The other main current is represented by Fidel Castro and Hugo Chávez, its most prominent figures. Between these two personalities, and between the political movements that sustain them, there are important differences, and it would be a mistake to compare them. Though however closely or remotely they may be connected today, they nevertheless comprise the Latin-American pole of the archaic left wing, which is still associated, by Fidel's grace, to that which was a world communist movement, a faded reflection of the light of the Soviet star, which is now extinguished.

These two left-wing currents coexist in the continent, and even though they could superficially be taken as being of the same "family", the contradictions that oppose them are quite evident. The Brazilian PT, Chilean socialism, the Uruguayan *Frente Amplio* and *Peronismo,*[12] all come from a long struggle against ferocious military dictatorships, and in the previous half century they have

---

[12] The government of Juan Domingo Perón (1946–1952) in Argentina was one of the most progressive in Latin America in the twentieth century—instituting the *Movimiento Nacional Justicialista*—hence the term *Peronismo.*

gone through the most varied experiences. These range from working underground, episodes of armed struggle that involved some members of various political parties (especially in Brazil, Uruguay and Argentina), participation in parliamentary life, the exercise of regional and local government, and even a national government in the Chilean case. Deep-rooted in the history of the continent, the already more-than-secular social struggles, which have reflected on their own intense political practice and "real socialism", have driven these parties to leave behind simple left-wing thoughts and to internalise democratic values as components *sine qua non* of the projects of social change. The single-mindedness—so characteristic of the cult of Lenin, Mao and Fidel—is already known to have produced mistakes, such as "the ten million tons of slag" in Cuba, or in "the great leap forwards" and "the cultural revolution" of the Maoists, not to mention the *tour de force* which was the Bolshevik revolution. In the economic field, having suffered the consequences of our mistakes, and especially someone else's mistakes—notably those inherited from the Soviet model—it is well known that the macro-economy can take terrible social revenge when it is handled in an unscrupulously and irresponsible way.

Leaving aside the radically false stridency of the "Bourbon"[13] left wing (of which, as in the Bourbon royal house, you could say that it doesn't forget and it doesn't learn), the "other current", which was previously mentioned, is the path of advanced reformism. It is one that makes social sensibility compatible with the understanding that the transformation of society requires it to undergo equitable economic development, and for democracy to be strengthened and deepened. Without the second aspect, any preoccupation with the social situation will be shipwrecked in the turbulent waters of inflation and economic stagnation or, as in the Cuban case, in a totalitarian dictatorship that functions as a mechanism of social control and survival through power. This only accentuates the autocratic dictatorial system, which is invariably accompanied by a failing economy.

Nevertheless, this kind of left wing cannot escape from the permanent tension inherent in the compromise between ideas and the pragmatic, which forces a realist perception of the surroundings in which it acts. Such tension feeds incessant debate, which, if we look at the historical background, surmounts those of the First and Second International.[14] This debate has often produced divisions and schisms in the parties in which these tensions incarnate.

In Brazil, the PT is constantly going through internal debates, which are always followed by minor divisions between the party's ideological mainstream and its extremist tendency. It is evident that the people running the PT understood early on that to avoid the "road to crucifixion" suffered by Allende in his dealings with the Ultras, it was necessary to adopt an attitude of firm

---

[13] See footnote 2.

[14] This is a reference to the organization of what was to become the Communist Party, in the First International (also known as the "International Workingmen's Association) (1864–1889), and the Second International (1889–1916), which is also known as the Socialist International.

intransigence towards extremists. Consequently, the *petista*[15] ultra-left wing chose to set up their camp apart from the mainstream, which was fortunately the best course of action they could have taken in regard to the Brazilian political process, a process marked by advanced reformism pursued by the PT and Lula. In Uruguay, Tabare Vasquez's first steps point in the same direction as those of Lula and Lagos, and not in the direction of Chávez. It wouldn't be surprising if the PT's northern neighbour, *Frente Amplio*, goes through similar arguments. Argentina constitutes a special case because *Peronismo*, which is globally recognized, does not have a left-wing affiliation. However, if we consider Argentina's current political leaders and we start with Kirchner, who comes from the "guerrilla" left wing, Argentina could today be considered as a member of the multi-hued group of socially-minded, cutting-edge governments that we currently see in our continent. It is improbable that anything near to the contradictions inherent in the "classic" left wing will emerge from *Peronismo*. In Chile, Pinochet's military coup and his dictatorship made the nation pay the cost of the "revolutionary" excesses of the ultra-left wing. It is the memory of that which has acted as a kind of vaccine that protects Lagos' government. Lagos hasn't had to battle, as Allende did, with the unproductive provocations that come from ultra-radicalism, which in other cases has contributed enormously to paving the road to a fascist revanchism.

Finally, within this "great current", there are other more moderate paths—which lean more towards the political centre, and which are a lot less subjugated to the ideological disjunctions that characterize the previously mentioned cases—specifically, the Dominican Republic's PLD, the Panamanian PRD and the PPP (*Partido Popular Progresista*) from Guyana. The first manifestation of this "great current" is to be found in the driving force of the sober, centred and unperturbed leadership of Lionel Fernandez of the Dominican Republic, which has put him twice in government. This current has emerged from the political and social turbulence that followed the disappearance of the *Trujillato*,[16] in other words from the electoral victory of the PRD, the military coup, the American invasion, Caamaño, Balaguer's governments, divisions in the PRD, and the birth of the PLD. The Panamanian PRD is an heir of the *Torrijismo*, and is now being led by the late Colonel Omar Torrijos' son, who is trying to link the sense of nationalism, which made "access to the Canal" possible, with social issues. (Omar Torrijos always said that he didn't want to enter history, he wanted to enter the Canal.) Social issues, by the way, were not among the priorities of the first Torrijos, but are now noticeable in Martin Torrijos' language, even though considerably overshadowed by an economic orthodoxy. The PPP in Guyana, currently in

---

[15] *Petista* refers the militant ultra-left-wing element of the Brazilian PT (*Partido dos Trabalhadores*)—hence the Portuguese acronym *petista*—one of the most important left-wing parties of Latin America.

[16] The term *Trujillato* derives from the name of the Dominican Republic's dictator Rafael Leónidas Trujillo Molina, who presided over a corrupt regime of terror for three decades until his assassination by disaffected army officers in 1961. Trujillo was behind a failed assassination attempt in 1960 against the reformist, democratically elected president of Venezuela, Rómulo Betancourt. In Latin America the name "Trujillo" has become synonymous with regimes of terror.

government, was the party founded by Cheddi and Janet Jagan. In 1953, the PPP gave birth to the first government in our continent to have relatively Marxist tendencies. However, it was ousted by Britain three months later; being one of its colonies, Guyana was still controlled by the British. Subsequently, the PPP has returned to government several times, but a barrier of language and culture has meant that the Spanish-speaking left wing have little or nothing to do with Guyana and, in general, with the Anglo-French-speaking Caribbean.

Given the historical circumstances in our continent, it is apparent that it is in this pragmatic, modern left wing that the prospect of advanced, sustainable and lasting social change lies. Its rhythm of implementation will certainly not be the same everywhere, but it will nevertheless probably continue to grow, each achievement creating the space for new and more fertile progress in matters of social equity and the deepening of democracy. All in all, this is just another way of saying: the creation of a just and free society.

The other important aspect of the Latin American and Caribbean left wing is the one represented by the outstanding figures of Fidel Castro and Hugo Chávez. The romantic appeal of this kind of left wing—with the consequent shots of adrenalin that *Castro-Chávismo* produces—finds its echo in some countries where the left wing seems to be ready to take power: in Nicaragua, Bolivia and El Salvador, as well as in the small groups from the continental ultra-left wing, and the even smaller and what could be described as fossilised "old communist" groups. We should also include some of the continent's social movements, such as the Argentinean *piqueteros*[17] and the Brazilian *sem terra*.[18] However, despite the diffuse sympathy that these parties and movements may well awaken in people who live outside the direct influence of these political groups, they do not engage with the main current of the South-American left wing. Regarding Fidel's "Palaeolithic" revolution, there is not much that we could add, but Venezuela's confusing "*Bolívarianismo*"[19] is attracting a great deal of attention, as it seems to possess a capacity for expansion that was lost long ago by the Cuban Revolution.

Nevertheless, we could perhaps agree on a few points of clarification concerning the three countries where *Castro-Chávismo* has its marginal supporters. In El Salvador, the FMLN is not only the biggest political group in parliament but has also taken over in the majority of the municipal councils. However, it denied itself victory in the presidential elections. By supporting the particularly sectarian candidacy of Schafik Handal, the general secretary to the Communist Party in El Salvador, the FMLN couldn't create an opening in the political centre and it limited its own reach. Without a doubt, Handal was a gift

---

[17] Meaning "picketers", the term refers to a social movement amongst the poor of Argentina who are mounting blockades (occasionally violent) of roads to draw attention to their plight. The movement properly began in June 1996. They are creating a new social network for the homeless.

[18] Meaning "landless", *Sem Terra*, also known as MST (*Movimento dos Trabalhadores Rurais sem Terra*), is a movement that was officially founded in 1984 to fight for the poor and for agrarian reform.

[19] See footnote 3.

from the gods to the declining right wing of that country, as there is an internal current within the FMLN that identifies itself with Chávez. The future will tell whether the party manages to gain control over the communist *apparatchiki* or, on the contrary, remains their prisoner. The future of the FMLN depends on the outcome of this contradiction. If the conservative—or "religious" left, as cleverly articulated by Joaquin Villalobos—manages to maintain control over the party's machine, then its decline will be inexorable. On the other hand, its arrival to power will also probably be inexorable.

In Nicaragua, even though the Sandinista movement (or FSLN: *Frente Sandistina Liberación de Nicaragua*) looks like the main political force of the country, it has gone through an accelerated process of ethical and political breakdown, which has generated doubts concerning what we should expect from their government, should it win the elections. The FSLN also produces a dilemma for the two left wings. In the Sandinista movement—which, more exactly, should be called *Danielismo*[20]—Fidel's imprint is very deep, and for that reason it shouldn't be a surprise that it aligns itself with *Castro-Chávismo*. However, it is obvious that at its core there is an unresolved struggle between the two left wings, most recently exemplified by the episode that resulted in the expulsion of Herty Lewites, ex-mayor of Managua, and in more distant past—although it didn't then create major consequences to the party—the expulsion of Sergio Ramirez. Nonetheless, today the contradiction seems to be deeper than when Sergio Ramirez challenged Daniel Ortega's leadership.

In Bolivia, Evo Morales' MAS has consolidated itself as the most important political force in the country, and its connections with the Venezuelans' cult of Chávez are well known. MAS has the interesting characteristic of constituting the first autonomous, political expression that has been made by the indigenous population— which is the majority of the population in Bolivia—even though it always played an ancillary role with respect to political forces in Bolivia. The emergence of MAS, which marks a turning-point in that country's politics, has produced the deepest social and political process that Bolivia has ever known. In the 1952 revolution, it was certainly the indigenous people who were the object of the reforms favoured by the MNR (*Movimiento Nacionalista Revolucionario*); and now it is they who emerge as characters in their own history. Understandably, in their political culture we find a mixture of modernity and retrograde thinking. Also, the many centuries of oppression, submission and humiliation that they have endured could explain their radical attitude on some issues—they are still, as it were, showing the scars of a previous affliction—and also explain their identification with the Castro-Chávista revolutionary paradigm. In times to come we will see whether MAS transcends its own ethnicity and manages to realize itself as an integrative force for the diverse, ethnic society of which it is a part—in the same way as did the African National Congress under Nelson Mandela's leadership—or whether MAS will end up being trapped as an indigenous cult,

---

[20] Deriving from the name of the Nicaraguan, Daniel Ortega (b. 1946), who joined the urban resistance movement FSLN in 1963 and became its leader. In the Nicaraguan national elections held in 1990, the FSLN lost to the UNO (Union of National Opposition), and Violeta Chamorro replaced Ortega as president.

crystallizing a dangerous, racial fracture in Bolivian society, which would entail unpredictable consequences in a country that is so complex and complicated, and in addition would entail MAS becoming a prisoner of centrifugal tendencies that could threaten its own territorial integrity. Incidentally, Brazil being a neighbour with whom Bolivia shares such extensive interests, it would be advisable for Lula to develop a close relationship with MAS and Morales, which could help coax him away from false radicalism and bring him closer to the attitudes of the modern left.

Within this context, it is perhaps necessary to add a few words about the significance that would be entailed in the eventuality of an electoral victory in Mexico for Manuel Lopez Obrador, who will almost certainly be a candidate for the PRD. It won't be easy for him to win, but it wouldn't be a surprise if he does; in fact, he is currently in the lead in the presidential polls. Despite the Mexican right-wing tendency to compare AMLO (the party of Andrés Manuel López Obrador) to Chávez, both countries' circumstances are so different that this tendency to compare the Mexican government with the Venezuelan government is simply foolish, misleading the gullible. But there is no doubt that a left-wing presidency in that other great Latin-American country would mark a qualitative leap in the politics of the hemisphere.

It remains to say something about the cult phenomenon of Chávez. This cult, for want of a better term, has emerged out of a confluence of nationalist militarism—which contains various currents that derive from the shipwreck of Marxism-Leninism—and the factionist left. It has the form of a movement and is represented by a government that is essentially selfish, with strong militarist, messianic and authoritarian characteristics. It is shaped by language that has clear resonances with Fidel's cult, which dates from the nineteen-sixties, and echoes through the ranks of the impoverished masses of Venezuela. Ideologically, for support, it purposefully uses the powerful cult-myth of Bolívar, which represents a kind of Venezuelan secular religion. People in the other countries of our continent, where the notion of a libertarian hero has not made the deep impression that it has made within the heart of Venezuela, find this hard to comprehend. Paradoxically, Bolívar's memory has been cultivated for over a century, especially by our "strong men" (*caudillos*), as a way to legitimate their abuses, with the support of Simón Bolívar's ghost. The contorted paths of collective frustrations are deeply ingrained in the popular psychology of Venezuela. Others have used Bolívar as a political tool as well, but no one has done it with the strength and efficacy that Chávez has.

The "Bolívarian" discourse has until now been tied to a vague and mostly emotional notion of social redemption, but more recently an attempt has been made to give it greater conceptual depth. This has been done by whimsically and grotesquely associating "Bolívarian heroism" with the attempt to find specific content for "twenty-first century socialism", which although practically indescribable has nevertheless been appropriated within the world of Hugo Chávez. Although his speeches throughout the last six years have derived from his attempt to establish the Bolívarian ideal as one that is "humanist", they have also resorted to Christian imagery, to anti-neo-liberalism, then to anti-capitalism, and just recently Chávez has arrived at the idea of "inventing twenty-first century socialism". All of this has taken place against a backdrop of nationalism, which has now tilted towards a strident anti-imperialism in the style of Fidel Castro, which is all within the context of a growing verbal confrontation with the Bush administration. However, and we must be clear about it, the main element of the cult of Chávez is his vigorous and charismatic leadership. As a bonus, this cult has been generously lubricated by the price of oil, which has reached astronomical levels. As a consequence, he has been able to build an effective and emotional tie with millions of Venezuelans on a level that on occasions comes to close to the magico-religious.

Government policy is ambivalent: Chávez swims in two waters. One is the water of democracy, as a strong culture of democratic traditions in the country constrains him. This culture is also informed by the influence of the inter-American environment, maintaining the formal characteristics of democratic life (consisting of political parties, syndicates and a plurality of labour unions, freedom of expression, etc.). The other water is that of authoritarianism, where the formal "physiology" of democracy is being undermined by an ever-growing, harsh and autocratic exercise of power (consisting of state institutions under absolute presidential control, a tendency to obliterate the areas where democracy operates, constant pressure on the media, and a tendency towards the exercise of "justice" by the police, etc.). Chávez's government isn't one that is either dictatorial or totalitarian, as in the Cuban case, but nor is it a democracy. It is authoritarian, militaristic, with strong autocratic tendencies. The affirmation of his personal power is the *alpha* and *omega* of Hugo Chávez's behaviour, which has made loyalty to the chief the touchstone of his politics.

The concentration of power in Hugo Chávez's hands is only comparable to the leading role played by General Juan Vicente Gómez, our dictator for twenty-seven years (which, by the way, does not imply a similarity in other respects). Military formation is not naturally democratic, but instead has its roots in the force of vertical discipline, and operates through tiers of subordination between one commander and others, and involves procedures being followed without thinking. This kind of organization converges with the dictatorial, authoritarian and non-democratic tradition of the Bourbon left. In sum, this produces the peculiar regime of Chávez, where the president is not the first among his peers but instead has become a venerated totem, who has the first and last word on all governmental decisions. As might be expected, the atmosphere around the leader has become thick with adulation and fear, becoming more and more repugnant. So, if it is about "inventing socialism", if we consider all that has been done so far in that regard, we are perhaps permitted to conclude that what has emerged is indicative of models that have previously failed, rather than indicative of a model of an alternative socialist democracy. Even if Chávez doesn't become a clone of a typical autocratic leader, he will still nevertheless maintain the ambiguity, although to a lesser degree, which characterizes him today.

Although Chávez has been successful, at least until now, in his attack on the old socio-political establishment in our country, which has destroyed its privileges, the fact that this has not taken place within a context of an alternative social project has inevitably resulted in the appearance of a new class of privileged politicians and even the beginnings of a new middle class, the so-called Bolívarian bourgeoisie or "Bolí bourgeoisie", who have emerged on the back of corruption and their business with government. Nonetheless, the government has both confronted and defeated the previously dominant powers, and has created popular appeal for itself, deriving both from munificence and its distributive policies (the oil cornucopia goes far). By employing a political and social discourse that lies somewhere between the redemptive and the revengeful, it has managed to establish itself deeply in the popular imagination of Venezuela. It is undeniable that Chávez has placed the issue of poverty and the fight against it at the centre of national policy. In addition, the practical implementation of a set of social programs—the famous "missions", some of which have an undeniable conceptual validity—have reinforced, without a doubt, the link with some sectors of the general population, even though how these policies are being applied is unclear, tinged as they are with the suspicion of corruption and favouritism. Within these sectors, it is evident that Chávez's government is for the poor, by the poor and of the poor. Since man does not live by bread alone, the feeling for Chávez feeds a need of a great swathe of the population, the masses who have been frustrated and disillusioned by years of abandonment and injustice. The point is that beyond the social programs there is not, at least until now, a policy for tackling the structural causes of poverty; and this is the Achilles' heel of the Chávez project.

During this past year (from 2004 to 2005), Hugo Chávez has introduced a new twist into his speeches, which previously was almost nonexistent: namely, verbal attacks on the Bush administration and "Yankee imperialism". As a matter of fact, for two years Chávez avoided any public accusations of Bush's government's involvement in the *coup d'état* of April 2002. He handled the matter with extreme caution, avoiding any direct accusations. Today, however, his accusations concerning the affair, along with some other paranoid ones about a supposed American plot to kill him, as well as the use of very harsh and sometimes highly offensive language against the president of USA, have become the *leit motivs* of his preaching to the world; he is responding to the very obvious attacks that have come from the American Department of State. It might be asked what has motivated these changes in the tone of the government of Venezuela, which was previously so cautious towards its northern counterpart? Could it be Chávez's aspiration to become an anti-imperialist leader of the continent, represented moreover by a leadership that is distinguished by a difference in style from other governments of the left-wing family, a leadership that tries to out-flank them on the left in order to draw out their internal contradictions? And is there perhaps an idea lurking in the background that the Americans will remain bogged down in Iraq? And could it be that Chávez then deliriously supposes that they would then be in their greatest moment of international isolation, so that they would have few options to oppose Latin-American challenges to their power, and would not consider any form of armed action against the sub-continent? Or, closer to home, does this simply represent an attempt by Chávez to reinforce his national leadership by means of an appeal to a "sacred union" against an external "enemy"? By the way, for Venezuelans this notion does not have the precision that it has for Cubans, and for this reason sounds hollow and somehow ridiculous in his long-winded speeches about the "asymmetric war", which we Venezuelans will supposedly wage in the immediate future. However, simultaneous with the verbal assaults on the Bush administration, Venezuelans are presenting a really bold form of external politics, even if it is extremely loudmouthed and provocative, in contrast to the serene and much more effective politics of Lula. Using his active personal diplomacy, which is being fuelled in a practical way by crude oil, Chávez plays on the theme of a "multi-polar world", all the while strengthening ties with Russia, China, India and Iran. Although he sometimes acts like a bull in a South-American china-shop, he has nevertheless also strengthened political and economic ties with Brazil and Argentina in ways that are beyond the mere rhetoric of regional integration. He has used oil as a simple political tool, which sometimes leads to extravagant gestures, such as in the acquisition of some of Argentina's debt.

Nonetheless, the exploitation of social resentment, the unnecessary creation of fear amongst the middle classes, the administrative inefficiency, the permanent conflict of interests, the political and social fragmentation of the opposition, and rampant corruption make the viability of *Chávismo* as a project of deep social transformation doubtful: it has become stagnant in the process of its own internal expansion. Chávez has not been able to bridge the gap with the people of the half of the country who oppose him. Instead, he continues to preside—although less infuriatingly since the referendum of August 15, 2004 that failed to revoke him— over a situation of social and political polarisation, which characterizes the period that began in 1999. *Chávismo* is certainly a popular force, but for the nation it is not a force of integration. In addition, there are disturbing signs on the horizon, which seem to anticipate an excessively implacable and quite undemocratic course for the development of the *Chávista* process. For these reasons it is condemned to fail; but to repeat Marx's own words: we must let the future speak for itself.

Despite their disagreements, among the two Latin-American and Caribbean left wings currently in power there are, however, numerous common links, and it would be premature to think that their apparent conceptual differences, and differences in their political style, would necessarily produce a fracture between them.

It is the modern, democratic left that has integrated the experiences of the armed struggles and the crisis produced by the Soviet model, as well as the misfortunes of *Allendismo* and *Sandinismo.* However, although this modern, democratic left does not mirror the Cuban model, its relationships with the Bourbon, conservative and non-democratic left are a feature of their management of their own internal tensions. Despite the fact that there is no real connection between them, both Fidel and Chávez are welcomed together with honours, treated cordially, and invited to appear before the popular masses. Tribute is paid to their myths, and they are considered to be part of a "family", even though they are like *enfants*—or better still, *pères—terribles.* On the one hand, this can all be understood as a form of loyalty to their own history. After all, we all used to be pro-Soviet and/or Fidel's followers, and all of us, more or less, went through the Marxist-Leninist cult; nor are we strangers to the intimate myth of Ché Guevara. On the other hand, but for the same reasons, this kind of behaviour is also a gesture towards the ultra-left, which is so often such a nuisance. This is in order to soften their protests and their belligerence towards governments whose policies, which they believe are too moderate, they condemn; otherwise, we would hear them say that we have "surrendered to imperialism".

However, there is also a factor that brings the two left wings together: American foreign policy in general, and in particular its policy towards Latin America and the Caribbean, especially now with Bush at the head of the current administration. The left-wing governments of the region, each one of them with its own style and goals, have a clear purpose to create new foundations for their relationship with the USA. But, of course, there are also considerable differences in style—as well as in substance—between the two left wings. Chávez delights in a vulgar style, full of bravado, when he responds to the frequent references to his politics by the American Department of State. He reproduces, within a completely different context and in different historical circumstances, Fidel Castro's understandably controversial discourse (Fidel has been confronting the terrible anathema of the Americans for almost half a century). But Chávez adds a few truly provocative improprieties from his own repertoire, which would be unthinkable in the language of the old Cuban leader, who is someone who knows how to "maintain his position" in such matters. Chávez starts from a false concept, which is characteristic of the old left: that there is no possibility of coexistence with the United States, which is the enemy *par excellence*. This concept corresponds to the ideology of the cold war, when all the communist parties of the world, and with them a small part of the non-communist left, used to assume the Soviet strategy as their own: that they were all set against the rival colossus. Bearing in mind their respective countries' national interests, they were incapable of developing their own policies towards the United States. For the new left, especially after the Soviet Union's collapse, this issue has become established in much more complex terms, which can be summarised in the following equation: that probable tensions will accompany an inevitable coexistence. In our continent, from the north to the south, there are many problems, such as drug trafficking, migration, terrorism, ALCA (*Área de Libre Comercio de las Américas*), etc., and there are different approaches to them, which are evident. But among these left-wing governments there is also the understanding that with a neighbouring country—which will be there until the end of time, whoever rules it—these controversial issues cannot be tackled from the perspective that they are "catastrophic", but should be solved by searching for mutually agreed solutions. The case of ALCA is a good example. While Chávez goes around with his loud-mouthed speeches about ALCA, brandishing a romantic, although non-viable and ridiculous "Bolívarian alternative" (which he calls ALBA: *Alternativa Bolívariana para nuestra América*, the Bolívarian Alternative for the Americas), Lula is successfully leading a constructive discussion, which does not aim to suppress ALCA but instead tries to adapt to the interests of both sides, for a win-win result. It is not by coincidence that Brazil assumes the leadership of the OMC (*Organización Mundial del Comercio*, World Trade Organization) of the emerging world, positioned as it is against the egoism and short-sightedness of the most powerful countries in the world. In one scenario, Chávez, the charlatan, speaks of putting up barricades, while in another he acts as a statesman. Lagos, on the other hand, has not hesitated in engaging the vibrant Chilean economy with that of America through a treaty of free trade. In the past this would have caused the Soviets to rain Jupiter's bolts of lighting down on their heads.

However, Bush's administration is not helping the development of a new, non-traumatic relationship. The arrogance generated by their own invincible power has prevented American neo-conservatives from overcoming the conditioned reflexes caused by the cold war. In spite of the attention paid to the Cuban community in the USA during the elections, a sort of Fidel phobia still obscures America's vision; they cannot manage to evaluate our current political situation except from the perspective of "Fidel's cult of subversion", a perspective which now, of course, is being boosted by the alliance of Cuba with Chávez. With a pertinacity worthy of better causes, different representatives of the State Department allow themselves to ramble on in public about the "negative force" that Chávez represents in the continent. To our leader, of course, this sounds like a kind of celestial music. He knows very well that the these kinds of statements will yield an abundant harvest in these suburbs of the world, namely nationalism and a sense of dignity in front of *gringos,* especially now, when Bush is the perfect incarnation of the "ugly American". In addition, Chávez is grateful for the opportunity that he has been given to be able to disqualify his adversaries with the stigma of being "imperialist lackeys". However, as far as the left-wing governments of the continent are concerned, their view of Chávez is much more complex and is not biased by American paranoia. So, they are not following a strategic line to isolate the Venezuelan president, but, on the contrary, they are trying to help to keep him within the democratic arena.

The Americans have not yet digested the electoral victory of the first Perón, which was accompanied by the polemical slogan "Braden or Perón". This election made the Argentines choose between the Yankee ambassador Braden and their leader of *Justicilista* (the political movement founded by Juan Domingo Perón). Also, the Americans don't seem to understand how it was that their ambassador in Bolivia, who made those stupid statements against Evo Morales, almost caused his victory in the presidential elections, which Sánchez de Lozada eventually won by a nose. They never realized that it was their ambassador in Bogotá, with his daily attacks on Ernesto Samper, who made it possible for him not only to finish his term but to do it with an overwhelming popularity of sixty per cent of the electorate. And finally, after half a century, the Americans have still not realized that Fidel Castro largely owes his prolonged stay in power to them.

In these conditions, in a continent where beyond the surface appearance the open wounds caused by a century of incursions by U.S. Marines from our coasts do not heal, no left-wing government in our continent can remain indifferent to the presence of American pressure and the initiatives against

Chávez and Fidel Castro. Somehow, whether or not we want it, with all its contradictions and misunderstandings, both Chávez and Fidel Castro are part of the leftist family of a Latin America that is looking to build a common destiny, and which opposes the hegemony of America.

Latin America and the Caribbean are giving birth to a new chapter in their history, which does not seem to be temporary and ephemeral. It is attended by the deep currents of social redemption, which flow through the dark holes of their unjust and iniquitous societies, causing the process to have a durable, democratic appeal. Whatever happens to the left-wing governments in Latin America and the Caribbean, this continent will not be the same as before. The hour has come for great social reforms, and this time whatever it is that is fully developing is not being determined or affected by the contingencies of a bipolar confrontation in the world, which is now history, but by the specific circumstances that have impinged on the continent's long and tortuous evolution.

Caracas, February–March 2005

## Chávez: the Bourbon left

After Gabriel García Márquez had finished writing up his interview with Hugo Chávez, a doubt was left hanging in the air: is Chávez really a revolutionary or would he simply become one of the numerous tyrants that this continent has produced? Six years later, Alberto Barrera Tyszka and Cristina Marcano, who researched Chávez's life and fortunes and written the book *Chávez without a Uniform*, ended up asking the same question: "Who exactly is Hugo Chávez?" And they have had to find answers for themselves by asking more questions: "Where does the history of this child lead, a child raised by his grandmother in a house built from palm-leaves with a dirt floor"? Is he a real revolutionary or a pragmatic neo-populist? How far do his social concerns really extend, and how much is just his own vanity? Is he a democrat who is trying to build a socially inclusive country, or is he an authoritarian leader who has hijacked the state and its institutions? Could he be both things at the same time? Who is this man who brandishes a crucifix while he cites Ché Guevara and Mao Tse Tung? When is he really presenting his true self? Which of those many faces is him? Which of those many kinds of Chávez is the authentic one? "It's not easy to know", say the authors. Nonetheless, somewhere along the way they have given us an interesting idea, which deserves our attention: Chávez is Zelig, the Woody Allen character who changes himself according to whoever he may be talking to. Indeed, this snake charmer, who tries to seduce anyone who talks with him, is Zelig. Whether it is a Catholic, a Muslim, a Maoist, a Peronist, a conservative, or even a Bolshevik, Chávez transforms himself according to who he is addressing, who could be the Pope, Jatami, Jiang Zemin, Kirchner, Chirac or Putin. In this era of Chávez, Venezuelans have become increasingly interested in pop-psychology; they try to gauge his politics by scrutinising the inner workings of his character. Although this somehow generally satisfies people, it often diverts attention away from the underlying motivations of this *homo politicus*, which, ultimately, is what Chávez is. This is because beyond all his personae, whether as the military man, the baseball player or the showman, Hugo Chávez is a politician; every one of his stage-performances is conscious and deliberate, strategically used to serve clearly undisguised political objectives.

This is how he is understood by Barrera and Marcano:

> It is evident that there is something in common with all of them [the many faces of Hugo Chávez]; it is a wish, an anguish, that motivates him, which doesn't let him sleep. It is an obsession, which—as happens with all obsessions—betrays itself. It cannot be hidden, whichever of his faces Chávez is presenting; it always wants power, obsessively, and more power.

This is, of course, the same character trait that any politician might value in himself. In that sense, there is no difference between Chávez, Caldera or Betancourt, just to mention the two most representative Venezuelan politicians of the second half of the twentieth century.

Betancourt is attributed with saying that "to want to be the president of Venezuela the first condition is to want to be president". If this is not true, it is certainly close to being true. Hugo Chávez could subscribe to this dictum without any problem. Apparently, according to the many testimonies of friends and relatives interviewed by the biographers, as well as Chávez's own testimony—which was discretely entrusted to his "personal diary"—from very early on in his life "he wanted to be president".

Why does he want power? Even for the most selfish leaders we can think of, power is never sought just for its own sake: it is never an objective in itself. There is always something beyond it that lights this kind of passion and makes it burn, even if sometimes the lustfulness inherent in the exercise of power, with all the concomitant dazzle and the related privileges, obscure the underlying motivations, which become diffuse and unrecognisable. Whether or not such motivations stem from the right or the left, or from a progressive or a reactionary perspective, they force some people, who take others with them, into the grind of the diabolical mill of politics. What Alberto Barrera and Cristina Marcano try to do in their book is to help us discern Hugo Chávez's motivations more precisely. Chávez's preoccupation with power is a sufficient reason, as explained previously, for us to try to examine and summarize the significance of some of the moments in the life of Chávez the politician in his struggle for power, and his ferocious fight to maintain it. This issue is thoroughly and objectively discussed by the authors, as far as is possible.

Throughout Chávez's shining career he has been helped by being underestimated by his adversaries and enemies. Only now have his opponents begun to realize that they are up against a formidable competitor. Not only has this underestimation been part of his good luck, but Chávez is also a lucky man. This description of him is not meant to be pejorative. On the contrary, good fortune does exist. Some people have it, and some people don't. This indescribable quality, which some people possess, has often made all the difference between success and failure. In an old American movie, *The Guns of Navarone,* a military chief chooses the commander of a team of soldiers who is going to infiltrate the German lines, and he voices one of the specific reasons for his choice, which he argues for decisively: the man has luck. Chávez, like Gregory Peck's character in that film, has luck. How else, for example, could the incredible chain of botched events of the 4th of February of 1992, which opened the doors to Chávez's fame and his road to power, be explained? This was when his captors, who were dishevelled, haggard and dressed in slovenly uniforms, were shown in visible contrast to the young official. They presented Chávez in front of the television cameras. He was shaved and dressed in an impeccable uniform, with his symbolic beret perfectly slanted; and he delivered a brief speech—which has now become almost mythological—which let everybody know that, true to his words, he would be back. In that brief speech he managed to consolidate the expectations and hopes of millions of Venezuelans. (It was like the shape of Cleopatra's nose for Mark Anthony: it was but a superficial detail, but one that changed the course of history.) It was lady-luck who then struck; the one who smiles on the audacious ones, as the ancient Romans used to say.

So, his luck has been underestimated. Chávez has twice surrendered himself since he began his political career. On both occasions, those who opposed him saw in his actions anything (including what they stupidly supposed to be cowardice) except his political sense, which is accurate and profoundly realistic. They made mistakes in assessing him, and those mistakes led to even more mistakes, which were deeply exploited by Chávez. Six years later, it seems that this has resulted in Chávez becoming ever more deeply embedded in power.

The first time Chávez surrendered himself was on February 4th, 1992. At that time, Venezuela's principal cities and military forts—Maracaibo, Valencia and Maracay—were still in the hands of his comrades-in-arms. Someone else, much less realistic or more adventurous, would possibly have allowed events to take their own course, and would not under any circumstances have asked his other co-conspirators to lay down their arms. The co-conspirators, as well as others, were of the opinion that Chávez should have fought. While some people maintain this opinion in order to underpin their accusation that Chávez was a coward, others say that this was purely for reasons of *machismo*. Chávez, nonetheless, that "impulsive madman", had assessed the situation before him very well. Having coldly calculated the consequences of the failure of his military action in Caracas, the only politically sensible thing to do was to surrender the republic's capital, which, besides being the main seat of power, also, crucially, garrisons the army. There was a failed attempt to capture the president, Carlos Andrés Pérez, who, for his part, had managed to mobilize the armed forces to confront the rebellion. Meanwhile, the entire national and international political world denounced the insurrection. (Ironically, one of the first messages of solidarity with Pérez, which repudiated the rebellion, was sent by Fidel Castro.) Clearly, Chávez understood that the three cities that still remained in the hands of his comrades were waging a dead-end battle and were condemned to defeat, and that a blood bath could be counterproductive to his political project. We have now mentioned a key concept: the political project. On the 4th of February Chávez was a man with a political project. To preserve the possibility of keeping it alive was Chávez's main priority; his life's project was directly associated with his own biological life. Chávez does not come from the same stock as Ché or Allende. He is not a man who would sacrifice himself for the sake of having his name in history. But surely, as any old plainsman might say, "while there is life there is hope". (This observation would also be true many years later, on the 11th of April 2002.) On the 4th of February he was right to surrender, but many friends and enemies criticized him for being a coward and even blamed him for the defeat. As related by Barrera and Marcano, Commander Jesús Urdaneta Hernández did not hold back from making contemptuous remarks about the president's manhood; and there was a definite reason why Commander Francisco Arias Cárdenas used a chicken as a symbol to negatively represent his electoral rival in 2000. But today Hugo Chávez is the president.

The second time that Chávez surrendered was on the 11th of April 2002. That night, considering the three options put to him by his vice-president José Vicente Rangel— to go to Maracay and get together with Baduel and to try and fight back, to sacrifice himself in MIraflores, or to surrender honourably—Chávez did not hesitate in choosing the third option. Chávez did not fight and he was not captured; he simply gave himself up, going to Fuerte Tiuna under his own steam. When he spoke to Rangel about the issue, after he had had a telephone conversation with Fidel—who also advised him to surrender if he could not fight—he concluded that the only logical thing to do was to give himself up. He called General Hurtado Sucre, who was by then his Minister of Infrastructure, and giving him his gun, laconically asked him to call General Rosendo to march him to Fuerte Tiuna. Once again, this was not a situation like that of Ché in the Bolivian jungles, or of Allende in La Moneda. This was nothing in this for the making of legend; there was nothing glorious or romantic. But, again, it was Chávez who was right and not the vice-president or the mayor of Caracas, Freddy Bernal. Bernal was one of Chávez's supporters and he publicly narrated the events of that day, thus shedding an unfavourable light on his boss. He said, without being euphemistic, that on that occasion Chávez had become totally depressed, and for that reason had not fought.

Of course, Chávez could not know that a few hours later he would be re-established in power, but that night when he evaluated the military situation in front of the members of his office, saying "Gentlemen, the military situation is disadvantageous", his diagnosis was realistic. Caracas was in the hands of the National Armed Forces (*Fuerza Armada Nacional*), who were demanding his surrender. To go to Maracay by land to join up with Baduel would have been an uncertain and dangerous adventure with unforeseeable consequences, given the overall military situation at the time. To sacrifice himself might have been an alternative for someone like Rangel, but not for a Chávez. Chávez was not yet fifty and had a different vision of both history and the future from that of his septuagenarian vice-president. By surrendering himself, the political project would be kept alive. In not signing his own resignation letter, he showed not only courage but also political astuteness: he had the vision of a commander who looks far ahead in an ill-fated time. Although he had been overthrown by a rebellion in a coup that was repudiated internationally, his government was nevertheless legitimized by a Democratic Letter from the OEA (*Organización de Estados Américanos*). This all took place in a country where he still had a great deal of prestige. Chávez did not have to look like a Perón, having to wait eighteen years to return to power. And in this respect you could think that, again, it was his good luck that accelerated his triumphal return and saved him from the interminable years that Perón had to wait. The rebels' mad insistency that he should not be allowed to leave the country, the threat to incarcerate him in a cage in the style of Abimael Guzmán, and the subsequent trial, made possible the bizarre episodes that would finally end up with the Armed Forces finding the perfect excuse to put him back in charge. These were the same Armed Forces who had asked him for his resignation, which he had agreed to; and all of this accompanied by the surreal incident of the non-existent signed resignation. (Did any of the overthrown Venezuelan presidents, Medina or Gallegos or Pérez Jiménes, ever sign resignations?). As we Venezuelans say, this was *pura leche* ("pure milk", meaning "amazing luck"). All this took place with Chávez knowing his partisans' movements, which was also a factor in the game, even though this didn't have the epic significance that Chávez later claimed it had. But, without a doubt, the decisive factor in the return of Chávez to the presidency was the attitude of the National Armed Forces.

On those two occasions, when it looked like he had reached his lowest point, his sharp political sense and the icy realism with which he assessed the circumstances allowed him to take advantage of his defeats, and instead transform them into political victories. From the 11th April 2002 onwards, his astute manoeuvres, and also the opposition's miscalculations, have made it look today as though there should be no significant obstacles on the road towards the 2006 elections in two years' time. The Chávez who came back to Miraflores on the 13th of April understood perfectly clearly that he needed a reconciliation with the forces that had overthrown him. It was evident that at the core of the National Armed Forces there was enormous discontent, and that it was not the Praetorian Guard that he had imagined it to be. The middle class had shown a tendency to fight and a capacity to mobilize, which he had not expected. At that time his government and his political movement were somehow "frothy", without organic roots that reached into society. So, he tried to repair the mistakes that had taken him to the brink of the abyss from which he had almost miraculously escaped. To this end, he took a step back and launched a conciliatory political strategy. By the way, the opposition did not come out to confront this strategy, as by then they were preoccupied by a series of issues that had resulted from the coup, and which made any form of dialogue or dissent impossible within the political climate that prevailed. On that occasion Chávez reinstated the managers of *Petroléos de Venezuela Sociedad Anónima* (PDVSA), who he had publicly fired on television. He asked for "forgiveness" for his actions, and somehow even consulted them about the company's new presidency, which resulted in the appointment of Alí Rodriguez, who at the time was not considered at all badly by those who would later be called "The Oil People". He made profound changes in appointments to various offices: he fired Giordani, Adina Bastidas, Rodríguez Chacín, and Dávila, all of whom had been significant figures in the administration; as a concession to the National Armed Forces he removed José Vicente Rangel from the Ministry of Defence; he nominated Tobías Nóbrega as Minister of Finance, which was obviously a move to please the economic sector, with whom Nóbrega maintained a good working relationship. Chávez also created a "Commission of Dialogue", which wasn't very successful, particularly because it was designed so badly. In addition, he promised not to wear military uniform; this was obviously a concession to FAN, as his wearing of a uniform during political events was felt very badly, even by his partisans. He ended the practice of universal and simultaneous broadcasts of his speeches by all the radio and television outlets, and significantly toned down the content of his speeches (which, as we had seen, had had a considerable influence on the conflict). As I have already said, the opposition was still obsessed by the idea of finding a way out through violence, and was preparing itself for a new round of insurgence. The opposition did not want to engage with his politics, and a few months later an atmosphere of civil war had again taken hold of the country. Chávez resumed his often-brutal fighting-style, meanwhile going ahead with a profound "cleansing" of FAN, which, ever since he did it, seems to have assured his fierce control over them. He sacked anyone suspected of not being fully engaged with him; and those who fully supported the "project", and especially those who supported him—including generals, admirals and even corporals—were put in high-ranking positions.

It has been argued that all of this was definitely done with the sole purpose of gaining time, and that the president's attitude was not exactly "sincere". Although, of course, sincerity is not exactly a "blue chip" in the political stock market, nevertheless, in any case Chávez's attitude needed testing. He was being challenged in areas of common political interest: a less traumatic process of evolution and a real sharing in the political life of the nation were needed, as was the need to stimulate the more moderate aspects of the Chávez cult; much good could have come if the president had stepped back in some way. None of this happened; but this is not the part of the story that we are trying to examine. Instead, we are attempting to bring to the fore the mistakes that Chávez said he wanted to amend, and to go back over other aspects of his behaviour, all of which have a lot to do with the profound political crisis that burdened the country between 1999 and 2004, which has not yet ceased, even though it is now considerably attenuated.

Let us for now leave aside the "help" given by the opposition, and let us return to Chávez himself. Chávez very nearly lost power on the 11th of April 2002 because he had dug himself into a hole that he fell in, from which he managed to get out by mere coincidence, or better still, by pure good luck. He has not hidden the reformative and revolutionary purposes of his government, and he has put considerable effort into an attempt to destroy both the broadness of his social appeal and also the alliances needed to sustain his purposes. All this only becomes understandable in the light of his immaturity, his childish attitude towards the left, and his impulsive "tactics". The great problem that confronts any social reformer is how not to "make the bed ready" for potential (and maybe inevitable) adversaries, through behaviour and conduct that create fear, apprehension and suspiciousness, which could all potentially tilt the "centre" towards an extreme position that is in opposition to the "reformer". Chávez behaved in such a way that he provoked confrontation with various sectors of society that were initially favourable towards him, and also with a few others whose neutral position it would have been useful to maintain. He provoked confrontation through his aggressive speeches, his sectarianism and intolerance when facing the opposition, and also through government policies that were driven from a ridiculously simple left-wing perspective. However, he did not really make progress on any great changes in the country, and did not create an organic political force with which to sustain his political actions in society. At the beginning of 2002, he had lost the battle for the centre. In 1998, the country had been mature enough to accept the institutional changes that gave back to the people the possibility of participation in the political processes, which had been confiscated by AD (*Acción Democratica*) and Copei (*Partido Social Cristiano de Venezuela*) during the time when only these parties were in power. The people were also mature enough to go accept important reforms, in the sense of reconciling economic growth with justice. Chávez's primitive and rudimentary left-wing speeches, as well as some of his political behaviour, generated fears, especially within the middle class—a significant proportion of whom who had voted for him—who started to feel alienated. This made it possible for the political and social sectors that had been displaced from government in 1998 to manipulate those fears from the perspective of the most intransigent form of anti-communism. After the collapse of the Soviet Union, such a course was essentially anachronistic and as rudimentary as the discourse of the president, but it was nevertheless an effective resource that was used against our unprepared and politically naïve middle class. In a few months the country had become dangerously polarized. For some, Chávez's government represented their social demands, justice and "vengeance" against those political parties that had ruled the nation for half a century; for others, Chávez's government constituted a dangerous communist threat, and the description of it as a "totalitarian dictatorship" did not take long to flourish. Powerful streams of adrenalin began to pump within an ever-growing atmosphere of irrationality, with Chávez and the media locked in a battle. This process was accompanied by scaremongering from both sides, and was plagued by wishful thinking and an incredible underestimation and ignorance of the "other", a process that quickly resulted in the substitution of careful analysis for political slogans.

The "ultra-left" rhetoric—which Lenin once described as an "infant's disease"—of Chávez brought the middle classes out against him and radicalized the bourgeoisie. These are the strata of society that are decisively influential on political behaviour in specific sectors, such as the military, the Church, labour unions, the media, and political parties. That is why, from the end of 2001 to the coup in April 2002, Chávez witnessed the emergence of an opposition movement, which in a few months made the label *escuálidos* ("the squalid ones")—which he used to use so contemptuously of his adversaries—seem like a joke; and it also almost got him booted out of power. Curiously, an atmosphere more properly associated with the years of the cold war was generated in our country. Over time, this atmosphere was further echoed in the typically stupid responses of the American Department of State. At the same time, their interference in our affairs strengthened the opposition, but paradoxically it also strengthened Chávez, as this interference allowed him to press "nationalist" buttons. However, seen with hindsight, one could conclude that Chávez's political actions during that period, which culminated on the 11th of April, were very clumsy. All he did through his behaviour was to create gratuitous enemies, as "bumper cars" for his style of politics.

Another interesting point is Chávez's relationship with the wider world abroad. The unnecessarily close personal relationship that Chávez established with Fidel Castro, and his hyperbolic eulogies to the Cuban revolution, not only created apprehensions in the middle and upper classes, but also were manipulated grotesquely, especially by the media. The result was that the "Cubanization" of the country became the great political issue. This created real paranoia in large sections of the population, who anticipated the imminent arrival of "*balseros*" ("Cuban boat people"). In addition to the clumsy and reckless way in which Chávez managed political affairs during those first two years, there was also the issue of the Colombian guerrillas, which became a media obsession for many long months, and which only heightened peoples' fears. Concerning both issues, Chávez had in fact not done anything substantially different to what had been done by any previous government. In the case of Cuba, when diplomatic relations were fully re-established during the time of Carlos Andrés Pérez's first government, they were preceded by cordial overtures. Moreover, Cuba has since then received Venezuelan oil. After Carlos Andrés Pérez had taken even greater political risks than did Chávez—for the obvious reason that the USSR and the "equilibrium of terror" still existed—he was able to celebrate a triangular agreement, together with Cuba and Spain, that guaranteed a supply of crude oil to the island. Concerning the Colombian guerrillas, contact was made with them with the aim of arriving at a *modus vivendi;* though as much was achieved between our armed forces and the guerrillas on our borders as was periodically achieved by our own governments. All of this was carried out, of course, with a very low profile and with the official consent of Bogotá. But in the case of preceding governments, no one in Venezuela had any reason to be afraid, since those governments were not sympathetic to communism and were not seen as a real threat. However, Chávez is dominated by a recently acquired and immature ideology, which he also projected onto Cuba and the guerrillas. He did not notice that he was already surrounded by a suspiciously left-wing aura, and instead of acting with prudence he behaved in a way that provided grist to his adversaries' mill. The flags came out in a call to action against the communist threat, mobilizing the gigantic marches in Caracas and filling the nights of half of the country with nightmares. At that time, the issue of the supposedly "communist" Chávez had a devastating effect on the National Armed Forces, the Church, the commercial sector and the media. In all those arenas, where a vast number of people initially viewed Chávez with some sympathy—or were at least neutral towards him—his popularity began to dissolve relatively quickly. This was not because of anything specific he done in terms of social or economic policy—in reality, he had done nothing—but because of the effect of strongly ultra-leftist and unnecessarily provocative rhetoric. There were also the famous forty-nine laws, proclaimed at the end of 2001. Although they were generally well received, and although almost all of them were innocuous, it was in fact these laws which were the spark that ignited the blaze in the camps of the opposition. The Land Reform Act itself did not go beyond the agrarian reforms of 1960, and in some respects it was less radical. But in the context of fears of "Cubanization", which Chávez himself so painstakingly awoke, this law added fuel to the opposition's fire. He provoked and conveniently manipulated the subsequent wave of terror, which engulfed the politicians who had been displaced from power, as well as the sections of the population who felt that the social and political privileges that had been forged over forty years—when the alliance between the great parties and the great bourgeoisie had dominated the national scene—were becoming endangered. On one occasion, some time before April of 2002, it was his right-hand man, Luis Miquelena, who told him that he had deceived half of the country with a fake revolution, and had scared the other half, who believed it was imminent.

But to the mistakes that Chávez made, from the point of view of what could have been conducive to real social change, we can also add those of the opposition, which did not lag behind. It was like a mirror game. Although the opposition was sufficiently strong to confront the government's administration, which was weak in many departments, the opposition did not realistically know how to manage the country's economy; it was happy to continue, diligently but uncritically, with its orthodox policies. Yet the government's opposition slid into the terrain of ideology, which was most convenient for Chávez: he could then identify *all* those who were his adversaries, many of whom had contributed, either by action or omission, to the confusion that Chávez himself had created among those of the population who had defended their own political interests and socioeconomic privileges, which the country had voted against in 1998. The "right" defined a stark opposition between themselves and the government, which they called *Castro-Chávista* and a "totalitarian dictatorship": both sides were now as equally opposed ideologically as the other. Naturally, any course of action was acceptable in a situation where, according to the arguments at the time, we were faced with a "totalitarian dictatorship", which, should it continue, would "destroy the country in six months". So, the opposition, which was dominated by its most extremist and radically conservative elements, and which comprised political parties that had virtually collapsed, were left with little or no capacity to determine the course of events: they allowed themselves the adventure of the coup. However, the attempted coup failed in April 2002; this was followed by an unjustifiable attempt to occupy Altamira Square, and then the oil strike. The only result was the reinforcement of Chávez's power. But 1999 to April 2002 were the years of a naïve "left". Years of mistakes reduced his socio-political base and almost cost him power. But then "another" Chávez emerges: one of the characters who Barrera and Marcano have helped us identify, someone who is more conscious of what is required to make "a peaceful revolution" (which is indeed an oxymoron), someone who is more pragmatic. He hits out but also negotiates; this was demonstrated during the prolonged negotiations of the OEA (*Organización de Estados Americanos*): he did not get up from his seat even during the oil strike.

The coup in April 2002 and the subsequent military insurrection on the 10th of October, which was followed by the occupation of Altamira Square (by the same military group whose core were the people who initiated the April 11th coup), gave Chávez the opportunity, as we have already mentioned, to go ahead with a complete "cleansing" of the National Armed Forces' (FAN) high command. High-ranking positions, from that of general and admiral to sergeant, were taken over by the president's men; not only by those who were ideologically engaged with him (who were a minority) but also by those whose loyalty he bought through undeserved promotions and a perverse use of the traditional mechanisms of corruption. Chávez regained a strong hold over the National Armed Forces, as demonstrated by the oil strike, when, opposite to what the military rebels thought, not one platoon moved a finger against the government. Throughout 2003–2004 he has been able to further consolidate his control over the organs of state. He covers his actions with a fig leaf of "democracy", which protects him, especially from the international community. Today, the armed forces are under such a regime of subordination that—without overstating the case, but not without good reason—you could talk of an autocracy. Legislative power, judicial power, civil power and electoral power; all these form a solid block of institutional power. Of course, it is not strange to find the ruling party in any democracy also having a majority in parliament; and as in the case of the United States, the Supreme Court is designated by the president himself. But while on the one hand there are functional mechanisms of "check and balances" in the "physiology" of democratic systems, on the other hand, the "philosophy" of an authoritarian system is precisely to nullify institutional counterweights. And Chávez proceeds in this authoritarian way, sometimes with caution, and sometimes rudely, unmasked. This enormous power became fully consolidated after the regional elections, consisting of practically complete control over the country's entire territory and political structure. This achievement did not go unnoticed by the opposition, who committed one of their biggest mistakes: they denounced a "fraud" in the RR of August 15th 2004, which they could not subsequently demonstrate. This accusation contributed to a large abstention from the elections by the opposition in the following regional elections on October 31st 2004, when Chávez's party won twenty out of twenty-two of the provincial governments, and 270 out of 335 of the disputed councils.

Another important consideration is that the defeat of the oil strike allowed Chávez to literally "privatize" PDVSA (*Petroléos de Venezuela Sociedad Anónima*). No private impresario manages his company with the discretion with which our president manages PDVSA. This company, for all practical purposes, "belongs" to him. We can imagine the enormous source of economic power that this represents, and the immense capacity for fiscal and economic action that this provides to the regime.

The sheer inertial force of the extraordinary amount of power that Chávez is accumulating creates serious dangers, as it leads towards authoritarianism and autocracy. In addition, he has other repressive tools of control, such as the Law of Social Responsibility for Radio and Television, and the reformed Penal Code (other such laws are pending), which were recently approved almost without any civilian protest, which is a clear demonstration of the public's deep retreat from front-line activity. The real characteristics of an authoritarian regime are becoming even more evident. Fear and adulation are thickening around the "supreme ego". The virtual absence of any institutional control over power permits the greatest incompetence among holders of public office; it permits unstoppable corruption and the most rampantly discretionary practices in the management of public life. The selfish and tyrannical nature of Hugo Chávez's power, which is supported by a disorderly populist revival, becomes increasingly more exposed.

However, the "process" is very complex. Chávez still has a strong, affective and emotional tie with the poorest and humblest people in Venezuela. It is a tie that lies in the echo of the notion of redemption, which, to them, does not sound in the least demagogic. The government's social programs, its famous "missions"—which are "messed up", "non-auditable", "improvised" and "unsustainable" according to the experts—have nonetheless reinforced that tie. The concept of "populism" does not have any negative connotation to those who are immersed in poverty and misery, some of whom, moreover, are receiving a modest but nevertheless widely distributed stipend to learn to read and write, or to study or to learn an occupation. And it must be admitted that there may be something to be learned from the way that these emergency social programs have been designed. In addition to the "missions", mechanisms of popular "empowerment" have been set up (such as urban land committees, water table monitors, cooperatives, and centres of endogenous development), which could potentially flourish in greater number in the poorer quarters and rural hamlets. If that were to happen, by the way, in the current situation it would eventually overwhelm the bureaucracy of Chávez's government. In some senses the country has profoundly changed, especially in everything that has to do with new levels of political participation and the understanding of its significance in the poorer quarters. Those involved with the phenomenon of *Chávismo*, which is still fermenting, are aware of this development, but at the same time *Chávismo* creates a challenge for itself, as it is administratively very incompetent and already severely corrupt. How do you manage an expectant people with a heavy and deficient administrative apparatus, which is disorganized and improvises, and which has so many civil servants of dubious integrity? On the other hand, among his partisans there are still a few who keep alive values of ethical and moral integrity, for whom the moral decay and corruption in some of the more sensitive areas of the regime have become abominable. It is becoming evident that the consequences of the murder of District Attorney Danilo Anderson[21] represent just the tip of an iceberg.

So, the regime is a tangle of contradictions. Some are already visible, some are latent. In a country with such a peculiar democratic tradition, one which forms part of the inter-American system—with all the duties that that creates—the necessity to make democracy compatible with what the regime calls revolution is not in any way insignificant. Another contradiction, which is potentially more prominent, is paradoxically the one that comes from Chávez's own strength and from the great expectations that he has generated among simple people. For now, Chávez's vigorous leadership can manage this confusion, but how long will it take before the inherent contradictions find political expression? Ahead of him, he now has two years of high crude-oil prices and the consequent potential for economic recovery (which the regime will opportunistically attribute to its economic policy, which will be arguable). This will no doubt contribute to greater political stability for him; though there are imponderable factors, and given a character as unpredictable as Chávez, these

---

[21] Assassinated by a car bomb in Caracas on the 18th November 2004, Anderson, the state prosecutor, was at the time investigating more than 400 people allegedly implicated in crimes against the Venezuelan state in the failed *coup d'état* of 2002. On 20th December 2005, three Venezuelan nationals (two brothers, Otoniel and Rolando Guévara, and their cousin, Juan Bautista) were sentenced to thirty years in prison for his murder. Some members of the Venezuelan government have suggested that the CIA may have been behind the plot; the investigation into his murder has not yet fully concluded.

can never be discounted. But it is obvious that a new type of opposition will begin to emerge from the ruins of the previous one, which will be all too familiar with the social, political and moral dilemmas that *Chávismo* carries within itself. How will Chávez confront this very probable prospect? Will he act as a democrat or as the revolutionary that he seems to think he is; as someone who tries to build a socially inclusive country or as an authoritarian leader to whom revolutionary speeches are nothing but a sign of his personal power?

I want to finish these lines by specifically pointing out that the introduction to Tyszka and Marcano's book that I have presented is somehow *sui generis*, in the sense that more than making a comment on the book, as is usually required, what I have done is to summarize my "story"—we all have one—of the Chávez who is presented by his biographers. Anyway, the initial conception was that it would be interesting to assemble both perspectives on Chávez, both my own and that of the authors of the book. However, I must say that in what has now become a torrent of biographies about the leader, this book certainly contributes important elements: it is the first systematic and fully documented biography; it is intelligent, balanced and unprejudiced. This great exposition of the leader's essential message was a necessary piece of work; it is a navigational chart, vital for understanding the peculiar phenomenon that is *Chávismo*, the cult of Chávez.

Caracas, January 19th 2005

## The physiology of the cult of Fidel (*Fidelismo*)

The book *America y Fidel (America and Fidel)* is a settling of old scores. In fact, Américo speaks of his writing as an act of internal liberation. We can understand him perfectly well. Américo, as well as many of his left-wing generation—among whom I count myself, more for reasons of idealism and shared struggles than for reasons of the accidents of fate and time—has gone through that searing spiritual process of suspending his own dogmatic beliefs. Only those who have been members of either a religious or a political church could understand how hard it is to abandon the dogmas that used to give our life certainty and reason. In the case of the Marxist-Leninist church, a certain internal strength is needed, and also a compromise with the values of freedom and justice, in order that disbelieving doesn't turn into cynicism or, even worse, a resignation to the world as it is and an acceptance of the dominant paradigms. However, becoming clear about our own self-deception—which for many people did not have to wait until the collapse of the Berlin wall—was somehow ostentatiously indulgent at the time, as we still had to deal with Cuba and what was going on there. Maybe the difficulty was partly on account of the "personal relationship" that we felt we had with many of these leaders, including Fidel; maybe it was because of what we could call our Latin-Americanism; or because we all share the culture of the Caribbean; maybe it was owing to empathy with the untamed warrior who does not surrender; or, most probably, the main reason was the residue of nostalgia for the revolutionary glow that dazzled us during the 1960s. Yes, there is a kind of loyalty to the memory of the tremor produced in all of us by those years of The Beatles, El Cordobés, the hippies, black Americans and their Black Panthers, "Black Power" and Martin Luther King. There was the glare of Vietnam and "uncle" Ho (Ho Chi Min), that revolutionary month of May in France, Algeria's FLN (*Front de Libération Nationale*), Frantz Fanon, Sartre rejecting the Nobel prize, the Latin-American literary boom, the years of Ché Guevara. Anyway, and maybe because so many of our best dreams remained lurking somewhere in the depths of our souls, we always managed to find a timely excuse for Cuba, even after we had discovered, more than thirty years ago, that communism was nothing more than a gigantic historical tragedy. Because it is in some sense "ours", because it is in Latin-America, Cuba was always somehow beyond (or maybe closer to) communism, and it has always had a place in our affections. Though, without a doubt, our affection for Cuba is a lot more for what it was in 1959 than for what has become today.

So, with this book Américo Martín simply engages with a process of what could be described as a dispassionate catharsis, presenting an exploration of the historical and conceptual roots of the phenomenon of the Cuban revolution. This event, like no other, left a mark on the second half of the 20th century, not only in Latin-America but also in the rest of the world, a world that has witnessed the central and quite extraordinary role that Fidel has played globally; and all from a tiny island with no more than ten million inhabitants.

The inquiry that the author engages with has a particular pertinence in our country today. This is because Hugo Chávez—who is more deliriously effusive than he is equipped with rational judgment—has established a debate, but one which has no proper context. On the one hand, his way of talking provided a basis for the fears (and also ignorance, it must be said) of certain parts of Venezuela's population, whose nights have been filled with nightmares of the Cuban revolution. On the other hand, he invokes that rather dull Bourbon left (which doesn't forget and doesn't learn), and which still resorts to the ancient imagery of mills and wheels.

For Chávez, Fidel Castro's arrival in Venezuela was not an act of superficial diplomacy (in fact, this was not Fidel's first visit to Venezuela), but an opportunity to exhibit an ideological position and stir up political confrontation. Some of the government's men, José Vicente Rangel among them, were conscious of how unnecessary and harmful such a debate was for the regime of which they were a part; they tried to stifle it, but in vain. Rangel, who was the Chancellor at the time, once said that when you have a situation where Madeleine Albright is visiting North Korea and Clinton is engaging positively with Vietnam, to oppose the presence of the old, bearded man was to be anchored in the 1960s.

Actually, the situation is exactly the opposite. The one who looks as though he is anchored in the 1960s is Hugo Chávez, whose pretence is to feed an artificial debate, one which is either in favour of or against the Cuban revolution; but this is happening when the brilliance of the revolution has already become a dying light, and when the inspiration that it once generated has now withered.

When Chávez puts the Cuban issue on the table, he insists on raising the issue of the identity between himself and Fidel Castro. Even though this irritates those on the right, nevertheless they are still willing to cross the bridge provided and to engage with the president. It also irritates the sensibilities of not only those who fear a Cuban "contamination" of Venezuelan life, but also those who are not reactionaries or paranoid, and who do not see the Cuban revolution or its social model as a good example of anything. Nor do they see anything in the old commander, who is now far removed from the ideal of a romantic guerrilla fighter in the Sierra Maestra, that irreverent rebel who inflamed the minds and hearts of millions of youngsters around the world during the prodigious 1960s.

All of this idealism disappeared for dark reasons of state, which went against the grain of what the anti-establishment world had expected. We all witnessed with amazement the support given to the invasion of Czechoslovakia, the silence after the Tlatelolco massacre,[22] and the obscene judgment and subsequent execution of General Arnaldo Ochoa.[23] There were, however,

---

[22] On 2nd October 1968, perhaps between 200 and 300 people were killed in the Plaza de las Tres Culturas in the Tlatelolco district of Mexico City. After several months of political protest in the Mexican capital, and a nine-week strike by students, the government cracked down hard on what was supposed to be a peaceful rally; the 1968 Olympic Games were due to begin ten days later.

[23] Ochoa (b. 1930) joined Fidel Castro's guerrilla army in 1957, rising to become a prominent Cuban general. He fought in many campaigns, and was behind a failed attempt to mount a

already unmistakable signs of the decline of the Cuban revolution or, even more, of Soviet influence, which effectively quashed it. The decline came about for many reasons: a totalitarian approach to politics, suffocating bureaucracy, the suppression of freedom, unlimited and indefinite personal power, a pitiful economy—for which the blockade was no longer plausible as an excuse—new and embarrassing social inequalities, a privileged social class, Ché's adventurous incursions into Congo and Bolivia, and the costly wars in Angola and Ethiopia. Fidel, the fierce fighter, has not been able to escape the inferno unleashed by the colossal planetary forces that he has tried to defy.

Fidel has been trying continuously to make progress for the last forty years. However, we are not trying to sentence him before we put him on trial. How many options did he have, being a prisoner of the bi-polar game that he so unwisely allowed himself to be dragged into? As Fausto, in order to save and assert his power, he sold his soul to the Soviet Mephistopheles; in the same way, he now sells it to the savage capitalism of trans-national companies, just to be able to survive. He doesn't prefer one or the other, but as he told Time magazine, he is a realist and knows how to swallow hard. The Soviet intervention in Czechoslovakia brutally shattered the thick veils of propaganda that had mystified Soviet reality. Those who had not wanted to believe it, those who still maintained an unshakable faith even after what had happened in Hungary, had started to admit it: the USSR was an imperial power similar to the United States; it didn't have friends or allies, just interests and unconditional servants. The "gulag" was not an invention of imperialist propaganda but was a sinister reality: it was brutal. Even the miserable abysses into which capitalism has plunged the former Soviet Union have been unable to erase the tragedy that was communism from Russian minds and also those of all the other nations of the fragmented Soviet empire. Their economic backwardness became obvious when the United States raised the stakes with "star wars"; the Soviet Union could no longer pretend: their economy was losing steam.

In Latin America something similar is happening with Cuba. Very few people still support the quite incomprehensible and unjustifiable American blockade of the island, which is an anachronism. But there are more than a few, including staunch enemies of the Cuban regime, who feel some admiration in the depth of their hearts when they see the adamantine integrity of the Cubans, in the way they have confronted the deep hostility of the biggest power in the world. Another aspect of Cuba's image, which is not at all insignificant to Latin-American sensibilities, is that when tiny Cuba is among the ten strongest countries in the Olympic Games, then millions of people feel that they are also represented. But there are no longer people in any social classes of our countries' societies who still see in themselves a reflection of the once exciting Cuban revolution. The old Cuba, abounding in history, legend and creativity, is today nothing more than a curio of political archaeology. A lot more dependent on sugar and tourism than before, its precarious economy sustains a stark social

---

communist insurgency in Venezuela in the 1960s. Ochoa was executed on 12th July 1989, after being found guilty of treason, corruption and drug trafficking by a Cuban military court. There has been some speculation that the trial may have been due to ideological differences with Castro.

division: of those who "accommodate" themselves to the dollar, and of those who "vegetate" with the peso. This produces a curious paradox: while the left denounces the "dollarization" of the economies of Ecuador and El Salvador, we find that in Cuba it is the dollar which is the real currency and not the peso; though, apparently, no one on the left is willing to admit it. Fidel's personal power negates any revolutionary idea. All things considered, Marx must be turning in his grave knowing that a personalized, policed and already calcified political system has been constructed in his name, one which is as far as it could be from the humanist proposal of popular self-government. Surely, seeing this, he would repeat what on certain occasions some of his followers made him exclaim: "I am not a Marxist!" Apart from the noble and heroic way in which Fidel and the Cubans have defended their country against the colossal power of the *gringos*, there is nothing salvageable from the Cuban "model." A good education system, or a good social security system, or being outstanding in sports (all of which definitely do not need of a revolution to be created), are not worth the enormous price that has been paid in terms of the loss of human rights, freedoms and the material conditions of life.

This whole scenario is explored by Américo Martín. The reader will also see the extent to which Americo's personal experience is found in his writing. His situation as leader of MIR (*Movimiento de Izquierda Revolucionaria*) and *in situ* player of our insurrection in the 1960s, allowed him to have close contact with the Cuban headquarters. The reader will particularly see how much study and reflection there is in the vast investigation that was carried out by Martín, and how a political, social and economic revolution, such as the Cuban one, was possible in the most unlikely place in the world, (something which Fidel has been repeating for the last forty years) an island in the Caribbean, 90 miles away from the Empire.

Américo finds that while one of the sources that inspires *Fidelismo* is Leninist thought, *Fidelismo* also has two other roots, one being Cuban history and specifically the politics of Cuba in the first half of the twentieth century, the other being the particular nature of Latin-American leadership. These currents, and the phenomena that distinguished them, converged in Fidel Castro's singular personality. He was Cuba's child of destiny, someone endowed with an overwhelming and charismatic personality, which is characteristic of all leaders who participate decisively in the formation of nations. In Leninist thought, Fidel found the ideal instrument to form a political movement, one perfectly adapted to the purpose of affirming and maintaining his personal power. Does he not embody the substance of all the main political institutions in Cuba? Beyond being the General Secretary of the party of the people—and not just of the working class, as postulated by the Marxist orthodox—he is the party. He represents the party's central committee, the political office of the central committee, and also the political office of the secretary of the party. This is all according to Trotsky's famous doctrine of progressive substitution, which with notable foresight and vision he defined as the logic inherent in the Leninist model of a revolutionary party.

Lenin would have made fun of "the constructive power of the people." He didn't believe either in the "powers" that he attributed to the party, that is to say to the community of "professional revolutionaries", or in the working-class status of the "general staff", which although entrusted to think for itself, could never possibly do so. From 1903, when *What is to be Done?* was published, Lenin established criteria to define the working class, a class which on its own could produce nothing more than syndicalism and reformism, and which could never produce a global, revolutionary vision of social change. This was the responsibility of the party, who were "the enlightened vanguard of the working class". It is also true, according to Marxist theory, that the party was destined to emancipate society in its entirety by emancipating itself. Nonetheless, Lenin would only discover that this would be his historical mission when it was pointed out to him by revolutionary intellectuals (the biggest percentage of whom, which Lenin never stopped mentioning, came from the bourgeoisie). The party would then be the incarnation of Rousseau's "general goodwill"; it would be a trustee of that goodwill, entrusted with it and beholden to it. The "mystification" of the party, the party *par excellence*, in other words the Communist Party, was slowly carried out. This was perceived with enormous perspicacity by Trotsky and Rosa Luxemburg. It consisted of the rationalization of a "proletarian dictatorship" as a necessary dictatorship of the "proletarian party", in which the general will of the proletariat was given shape. We have already mentioned what followed: those with "general goodwill" became disenchanted and their numbers successively dwindled. And we always find the same outcome everywhere: the party that substituted itself for the proletarian class was in turn substituted by the Central Committee, represented by the legendary Politburo. In turn, this process of substitution percolated through to the Secretaryship, and then to the almighty General Secretary: in other words, to a Stalin, a Mao, or a Fidel Castro.

América makes a fascinating exploration of this development, of what the party became: a tool of social engineering and regimentation. No longer was it the means to an end, but it became the end in itself. The party became identified with the state. Its military discipline, the subordination of militants, and the chain of command— from inferiors to superiors to the General Secretary—made the Leninist party symmetric to the armed forces. It is clear that the temperament of an autocratic leader could find in a party of this kind a perfect solution for his main concern: how to drive home his power and exercise that power without any counterbalance. In Fidel's case, by consolidating his position as General Secretary (or Prime Secretary, as he is referred to in Cuban terms), he amalgamates his other roles, as President of the Republic and Commander in Chief of the Armed Forces. Fidel, the leader, is like a clasp that grips all facets of Cuban political power.

Furthermore, Fidel did not buy into Leninist thought in the way that so many grey-suited *apparatchiki* of the communist world did. But by appropriating it, Fidel was able to exercise a type of control that meant that any of the *apparatchiki* could be dispensed with without incurring any resentment from anyone in the power structure. Fidel is a *caudillio* (a "strong man"), one of those characters who can hardly be captured in a single image. Leninist thought simply provided him with the political rationalization and the means of organization that enabled to exercise totalitarian power, in terms of ideology, culture, the police and the military. Fidel, the *caudillio*, certainly exercises power, but what power itself consists of is intangible and hard to define; some human beings exercise it with the sheer weight of their own charismatic personality (indeed, the word "charisma" means "gift of the gods" in Greek). In a continent where, still nowadays, a country's institutions may exercise hardly any restraint over someone's actions, Fidel Castro is one of a cast of Latin-American characters who represent historical points of reference: such people define the life of their nations—whether for good or bad—for long periods of time. In this sense, Fidel Castro connects with a tradition, one which Américo takes back as far as the Spaniards who tamed the new world, "full of sound and fury" in their extraordinary adventure, the conquest of America. Of course, a *caudillio* does not necessarily have to take the democratic process into consideration; he does not really need to consider democracy when he has a direct relationship with the people. Between the leader and the people the mediation of a political party is not always necessary. Even though it was necessary for Fidel to create a party, it was but for the purpose of providing him with a tool, a transmission-belt for his will power. It was not a properly influential body that could inform the leader's actions. The *caudillio* does not necessarily need a party; he may simply use it because his relationship with the people is direct: a *caudillio* may effectively be the plebiscite.

Everything else in the process was provided by the historical and political situation of Cuba itself, by the complex psychological and sociological peculiarities of a nation where the Spanish empire survived until the end of the nineteenth century, where there were the wars of independence of Bolívar and San Martín, and Cuba's own wars. These events were tragically followed by the crushing dominance of the young Yankee empire, which did not provide a practical solution for political continuity. We cannot very well understand the process of the Cuban revolution unless we take into account the fact that *Fidelismo*, more than a form of anti-imperialism, has been an expression of nationalism. In some way, Fidel Castro has been a son of the Platt amendment; a "sin" that the *gringos* have been trying to expiate for more than forty years.

Many thousands of pages and hundreds of books have been written about revolutionary Cuba and Fidel Castro. But Américo's book is neither a biography nor is it a historiography. What Américo has done is to present a political examination of the physiology of the Fidel phenomenon; an analysis of how this kind of Latin American and Caribbean totalitarianism formed and developed, and the significance that Fidel has had within it as the last great *caudillio* of Latin-America.

Having said this, which is a lot less than what should be said, it is now time for the reader to engage with Américo Martín's work. It is well worth it; it is a brave lesson about our past, and, essentially, it will provide a basis for understanding a future that we have yet to catch a glimpse of.

Caracas, Spring 2001

## Lula: The viable left

I

"From now on, everything that will happen will be to my advantage". With this sentence Lula ended the lengthy story of his life during an interview in 1994. The interview was for a book, *Lula: O Filho do Brazil*, written by Denise Paraná. And what "advantage" has Lula gained: nothing less than the presidency of his immense country, which is almost a continent. So this is how the epic career of this fifty-eight year-old has culminated; a north-eastern kid, the descendant of a father who was an illiterate coffee stevedore—and who was buried destitute—and a mother who was also illiterate, and who, in the words of her now famous son, "brought up five poor but honest boys, and three daughters who did not have to prostitute themselves to live".

The history of the PT (*Partido dos Trabalhadores*), which in no small measure is also Lula's history, almost looks as if it has emerged from one of the apologetic novels that preceded or followed the first few years of the Soviet revolution. You could almost believe that you were reading *The Mother*, the paradigmatic and now almost forgotten novel by Máximo Gorki. Arising in 1980 from the core of the São Paulo working class, and owing little or nothing to the intellectual bourgeoisie or to the middle class, the PT wanted to be the party of a group of trade unionist. However, when they visited the Congress in Brasilia they found out that there were only two labourers among them. The conclusion of the president of the powerful ABC (*Sindicato Metalérgicos*, the Trade Union of Metal Workers) of São Paulo was that "we have no representation. We have to create a working class party". His brother, Chico Frei—the only politician in the family, and a militant from Brazil's communist party—tried to persuade him with a typical argument, that the Brazilian working class already had a party (was he perhaps referring particularly to the legendary Luis Carlos Prestes' "party", the *partidâo*, "the great party"?). Lula replied that using the name "communist" would not take them very far. Curiously, ten years before that, here in Venezuela, the founders of MAS (*Movimiento al Socialismo*), had abandoned the PCV (*Partido Comunista Venezolano*) using exactly the same argument. In sum, this simple argument was an obvious and profound illustration of the defeat of the communists in Latin America, due to their long association yet sense of alienation from the Soviet Union, whose failure to provide a viable alternative to capitalism and democracy was clearly visible.

On the long journey throughout its various phases of organization, the PT has metamorphosized three times. Firstly, it stopped being a class-conscious party, and became progressively more of a national party. It was not only supported by poorer people and the middle class, but also by trade unionists and a brilliant intellectual and cultural elite. Secondly, although the party had appropriated some old left-wing currents, of Marx, Lenin, Trotsky and Fidel, it metabolized them, transforming them into the merely internal tendencies of a party whose mainstream ideology has over the years become what could be called social-democrat. (It should also be noted that in any South-American country that has terrible levels of social exclusion and poverty, there are very specific problems and solutions, which are somehow different to those that prevail in Europe.) Thirdly, before winning control of the central government, the party had already been putting its policies into practice through a few provincial governments as well as some of the most important city councils of the country (with notable success, by the way). In addition, they brought to Congress an ever-increasing number of parliamentarians. This has caused them to think realistically: there is a difference between leading popular demonstrations asking for aqueducts for the shanty-towns, and having to build them. They have learned how to govern and well know the limitations of "voluntarism".[24] In this way, the PT has arrived in government as a great national and popular force; it is pragmatic and modern and it has specific programmes, but it has not lost the decisive, redemptive spirit of the poor, for whom Lula is a real emblem.

II

A recent trip to Brazil, where I had been invited by the new government, allowed me to take a quick look at Lula's first efforts. Naturally, for a party of its kind, his initial steps have enlivened the contradictions between its modernizers and its ultra-left wing. In a previously published article we commented that if the PT could manage to rein in its most radical elements, then Lula's government could be successful. We remarked that this was very important, as otherwise the Brazilian right could become overwhelmed by paranoia. Listening to José Genoino, who is the party's president and also one of its "historians", one could hardly imagine that the Brazilian extremists could cause Lula serious problems similar to those that MIR and the Socialist Party's "extreme" wing created for Allende and his government in Chile. (It is also interesting to note that when Genoino was talking he also referred to the Venezuelan case of Hugo Chávez as a negative experience of radicalism.) Within the PT, the formidable influence of the well-organized working class carries significant weight, as does the sense of realism, which has resulted from the years of experience running local and regional governments: extremism now has very little breathing space in the inner workings of the party. But this situation could also be influenced by the fact that Brazil is a divided country, where an astonishing number of people are socially excluded and where expectations are great. Also, we only have to recall the tribute that the PT paid to the demagogy of Cardoso during the period of his government. Lula is now being forced by circumstances to adopt the grand economic and political policies of Fernando Henrique's government, the same policies that he dramatically denounced as "neo-liberal" when he was in opposition to the government. He is now seeing how those on the left wing of his party are beginning to change direction. However, they still largely remain anchored in (pseudo) revolutionary mythology and seem incapable of understanding that there are no free lunches, and that social change is not just a

---

[24] The concept of "voluntarism" is employed by Communist and Socialist theoreticians to describe the will of the people, which is a fundamental principle, and which works towards a co-operative society.

matter of will or good intentions. As was to be expected, the first shots against Lula's economic policies have come from the PT itself.

One issue is particularly revealing: a new law for social security. It is the first great project to be introduced by the new government to Congress. During a conversation I had with Arthur Virgilio, chief of deputies of the PSDB (*Partido de la Social Democracia Brasilera*, Fernando Henrique Cardoso's party), he told me that they were going to vote in favour of the law, but also that they had reminded the PT that it could have been approved two years ago if the PT had not blocked it in Congress, criticizing it as neo-liberal. There is a price that has to be paid by many political groups (not only on the left) for speaking in a certain way when in opposition: they often have to speak in a diametrically opposite way when they achieve government. In our own country, how many times have we seen the spectacle of AD and Copei in those contradictory roles themselves.

But, of course, the politics of alliance that the government is now engaged in are also quite unpalatable for the ultra-left. It already had to swallow hard when it was forced to form an alliance with the Liberal Party in order to win the election, which resulted in the entrepreneur José Alencar becoming vice-president of the Republic. However, this move was reluctantly explained as being merely a tactical manoeuvre for the elections. But now, with the opening of the PT towards the PMDB (*Partido del Movimiento Democrático Brasileño*, the party of the ex-president José Sarney, who was elected as president of the Senate with the PT's votes), the ultras provoked public dissent for the first time when Senator Heloisa Helena refused to vote for Sarney. But the PT's steps are perfectly logical; it is now far from the simple left-wing position which conceives of the processes of social change as inevitably confrontational, as though there were no tomorrow ("intensifying the contradictions", according to the old Leninist jargon, or "if it's worse it's better"); the PT is building solid foundations for governance. There is nothing really to search for on the left, as nearly all those on the left have joined forces with the PT. Even so, it still remains far away from a parliamentary majority, and this creates an opening towards the centre-right. One of the tragic mistakes of Allende's party was when it decided, but with only thirty-six percent of the seats, not to co-operate with other parties. They ignored the significance of the Christian Democrats, who with their share of the votes in Congress had facilitated Allende's election. The Christian Democrats could therefore have provided the factor necessary for stability. It was impossible in a democracy, as was illustrated in the Chilean case, to govern with only a third of the country in support, at the same time harassing the other two thirds of the electorate with extreme left-wing rhetoric and policies. The ultra-left approach polarized Chilean society and both political extremes, both the left and the right, and effectively blackmailed the moderates on both sides ("treason" was the cry heard from both extremes, who demonized any opening towards the opposite side). This made it impossible to achieve the agreements necessary to secure democracy and the viability of progressive reforms.

Of course, none of this has the romantic fire of the mania of the "myth of revolution"—which has ended up in so many failures—but it does have the solidity of a project which does not propose to "take the earth by storm", but simply aims to secure three meals a day for dozens of millions of Brazilians who do not currently get them. This could be achieved through a programme of progressive reform, even though it begins with a narrow margin for manoeuvre within the economy. Brazil's foreign debt will this year consume fifty-six percent of the country's budget, and for this reason what the government needs, above all, is the security of knowing that it can pursue its policies without any shocks other than those found in any other mature democracy.

Brazil, 17th January 2003.

PART II

## Bush's neo-conservatives and 9/11

As a consequence of the monstrous terrorist attacks against the United States, a universal phenomenon seems to be engulfing the world: it is a singular attitude, which considers any criticism of American policy, whether in the past, present or future, to be "politically incorrect". The stark dilemma presented by Bush ("those who are not with us are with them") leaves no option: if, at this present juncture, we don't uncritically accept all American policy, then we are with the terrorists. Should anyone express any doubt or reservation concerning the relevance of any aspect of American conduct, then they are immediately transformed into a "transgressor", into someone who is terrorist sympathizer; or at the very least their attitude generates an "ambiguity". The worst consequence of the current American position is that any criticism of previous foreign policy could also be considered suspicious. An entire machine of intellectual and political terrorism has been developed, which operates to degrade anyone unwise enough to dare to remember, for example, the day when Eisenhower's government decorated Pérez Jiménez.

In this short article I will be inquiring into the foreign policy of the United States, and will be approaching the relevant issues from three angles, hoping to avoid being inundated by new showers of criticism from those who might say that I am just rehashing old chestnuts, or that I am just like a stubborn goat behaving quite predictably.

The first angle concerns the charge that those who are not supportive of US policy support terrorism. This is not only morally unacceptable and condemnable, as it is couched in terms which do not permit any relativity, but is equally condemnable and unacceptable from a strictly political point of view. In the first place, this is because to create terror, even if it doesn't involve killing, is to attack some of the most profound values of the human spirit. Secondly, in the memorable pages of Lenin, who has already written about the issue, it is made clear that terrorism is politically ineffective and self-defeating. It turns against those who perform it. Regarding my own political life, all the old leaders from the PCV and the era of the armed struggle would corroborate how during the heated debates which I led, I objected to any action that definitely had a terrorist element. I particularly remember one which has followed me like *karma* for more than thirty years: the episode involving the train from El Encanto. I believe then that no one should think that if I say that Kissinger offered patronage to Pinochet it is because I am in agreement with Bin Laden.

The second angle is communism. I eventually finished my involvement with Soviet communism, silently withdrawing myself from the Communist Party, and leaving the reasons why I did it written in several books. I did it at a time when it was graceful to do it, the 1960s, when the USSR was at the height of its power and influence, and when the world's left wing venerated Fidel Castro. Nobody should think that if I now highlight the fact that the CIA sponsored Castillo Armas in Guatemala it is because I am in agreement with the "*gulag*", or because I close my eyes to the plight of the Cuban boat-people.

The third angle is the role of the *gringos*. I have to say that I am an admirer of the United States; I admire the genius and strength of its people, their sense of unrhetorical practicality. I love everything from their literature to their baseball. If there was anything that influenced me to adopt anti-totalitarian thought and caused me to break with communism, it was the powerful American democratic tradition, a tradition that allowed it to defeat its own form of fascism and McCarthyism with the sheer strength of their Jeffersonian respect for the law. If somebody were to ask me who is the political character I admire the most, I would immediately answer without hesitation that it is Franklin Roosevelt. But, if I repeat what he sententiously said, that "Somoza is a son of a bitch but he is *our* son of a bitch" it is not because I necessarily have any sympathy with the former Soviet Union.

Having laid out these angles of inquiry, I would now like to ask what exactly Dick Cheney meant to say when he asserted that "for this sordid war that is being prepared, and for the future, we must establish relationships with people whose very existence we find repugnant, who are depraved and without any ethical principles".

Does this mean a return to cold war politics, to the time when you could support any killer or rebel provided they were anti-communist? Somehow, in the past the "ugly Americans" always managed—often almost coincidentally—to support "repugnant people". It never—or only very exceptionally—supported social reformers, centre-left democrats or anyone who allowed themselves any sort of political autonomy. Having had to choose between Lumumba and Mobutu, for thirty years America supported the eccentric little tyrant who bled the ex-Belgian Congo in both human and economic terms. Are we then going back to the times when the CIA could ally itself with Manuel Contreras (who was previously chief of the Chilean secret police), in order to assassinate Allende's former minister, Orlando Letelier, in Washington's own streets?

The list of "depraved" or "repugnant people" in Latin America is long indeed, and each one of those names is drenched with blood. But they were anti-communist, and so it was valid to strike deals with them for that "sordid war". As Kissinger said, "the United States could not allow a Marxist regime in Chile because the Chilean people are simply 'irresponsible'". This line of thinking meant that they could strike a deal with someone as repugnant as General Felón.

Will those of the likes of Pinochet, Videla, Stroessner, Odría, Onganía, the Brazilian generals, the Ecuadorian generals, the Bolivian generals, Somoza, Ubico, Castillo Armas, Batista, "Chapita", Duvelier, Gómez, or Pérez Jiménez ever return to prominence? Will we ever see the return of such kinds of sadistic murderers, who were produced by our continent's political polices? Will we see the return of the likes of Suharto, Ngo Dinh Diem, or Ferdinand Marcos, or, in short, anyone who has been described as "depraved" or as being "without ethical principles"? Such people had, nevertheless, unconcealed guarantees of support from various American governments, but filled the life of so many nations all around the world with pain and death. Will current American policy breed similar vultures; will it sponsor a new breed of Noriegas, Montecinos, Husseins or Bin Ladens?

The great strength of America has to do with the fact that the most severe criticism and condemnation of the ugly side of America has come from themselves. Nobody has disclosed the various crimes perpetrated by the CIA more than the American Congress itself. But Cheney's words are chilling, particularly because one can easily see in them how morally supremacist thought is still very much alive. It is the kind of thinking that permits deals with despicable people who have no ethical principles, but one which is also accompanied with the peace of mind generated by believing that you are the incarnation of "good" on earth. It is incredible that anyone could believe that they could be an ally with people who have no ethical principles, and yet not realize that they are at the same time sacrificing or damaging their own ethical principles. Only the most dim witted fundamentalism could produce such criteria. This moral Manichaeism, which underlies all religious and political inquisitions, and which lies at the heart of all "ethnic cleansing", "final solutions" and wars, is extremely dangerous when, in situations of global conflict, it is assumed by the world's most powerful actors. The broken crockery produced by war is not only paid for by the enemies of this great superpower, but also by those who, although not really enemies, may be categorised as such by the USA, simply because they have a more sophisticated understanding of complex problems: they cannot just agree with the simple alternatives presented by George W. Bush.

Caracas, October 2001

## Chávez and Islam

The atrocious terrorist attacks on symbolic American targets have placed the issue of Chávez's government's relationships with Islamic countries in general—and with Iraq, Libya and Iran in particular—firmly on the table. Within our country, some sectors of the opposition have demanded that the government revise its foreign policy, the implication being that the government should at least distance itself from these countries, if not effect a complete rupture. Furthermore, this is not to mention some peoples' eccentric demand that the government should literally perform an act of contrition in front of the statue of Liberty, in the light of the government's *liaisons dangereuses* with the Islamic world and with Carlos "the jackal". Some retired officers from FIM (*Frente Institucional Militar*, Military Institutional Front) have managed to obtain a pronouncement from the National Armed Forces (FAN), which demands that the president change his politics towards some of the Arab states.

Let us then examine the issue. In Latin America there is no other country that has such close relationships with the Islamic world and the Arab countries as does Venezuela. The reason is easily understood: we are all producers of oil, and since 1960 we have together participated in OPEC (Organization of the Petroleum Exporting Countries). This cartel is effectively the world's only real cartel (apart from the drug cartels of the Third World, which continue to operate successfully, despite efforts to suppress them by the developed world). OPEC was created in 1960, thanks to the efforts and foresight of Rómulo Betancourt, whose colleague, Juan Pablo Pérez Alfonso, who was Minister of Mines and Hydrocarbon (which was the name previously given to what is today called Energy and Petroleum), was the great *in situ* designer of the oil agreement.

Since then, Venezuela has sustained a privileged relationship with the member countries of OPEC, because this organization, despite its changing fortunes, has remained the main player in the global oil game. OPEC is an organization riddled with numerous contradictions, and its members look at each other with suspicion. A few of them have confronted each other, even on the battlefield in very deadly and bloody wars. None of them, with the exception of Venezuela, is a proper democracy. On the contrary, among the Arab member countries, those which have not had a brutal and implacable military dictatorship—as in Iraq—are still mediaeval monarchies, as in Saudi Arabia and the Gulf emirates. Of the non-Arab countries (but which also belong to the Islamic world), Nigeria and Indonesia are two of the most corrupt in the world, and it is only now that they are beginning to leave behind long-running military dictatorships. Meanwhile, Iran, a theocratic state, is still agonizingly debating, struggling between modernity and traditionalism. Algeria, despite its authoritarian regime, comes nearest to the political standards of those of Venezuela. These are facts of reality, nonetheless. In a contemporary, "globalized" world such as this, there are debates over cultures and civilizations that are in many ways very far apart from each other. In the United Nations, the most developed countries live side by side with the most undeveloped ones. However, we are all part of the same world, and the reality of geopolitical games is that nobody really chooses either their enemies, allies or friends. Circumstances create different blocks of power, which are usually volatile and mutable, as are the circumstances themselves.

OPEC has survived many apparently insurmountable internal disputes: concerning the strategic differences between its members, the very often contradictory alliances that its members have developed—or are developing—with the world powers (Saudi Arabia is a safe and trusted ally of the United States; Iraq was an ally of the Soviet Union, and this is just to mention a couple of relevant instances), and the mutual stab-wounds that they have inflicted on each other. But no one has been able to kill off OPEC, not even Ronald Reagan, who boasted that the petroleum organization would be "brought to its knees".

Throughout the years of various governments (Social-Democrats or Social-Christians), the Venezuelan state has always maintained an unwavering policy of defence towards OPEC, which is perhaps the most consistent feature of Venezuelan foreign policy. Chávez has continued previous state policy on this issue, without making any changes. He has not done anything new. Since 1958, all governments have preserved this as one of the main axes of our foreign policy, which is an admirable demonstration of continuity in a country where each new government that takes over overturns whatever the previous government did.

Having said this, I must point out that in 1999, when Hugo Chávez assumed the presidency, OPEC was going through one of the worst periods in its history. Oil prices had dropped dramatically, down to eight dollars per Venezuelan barrel (in 1998 the average price had been sixteen dollars), and the cartel seemed to be condemned to collapse, as a consequence of the acute disagreement among its members, who were calling each other liars and of trying to cheat over the fulfilment of their own quotas. Through their efforts, Chávez's government made a very successful contribution to the situation, resulting in the re-establishing of confidence among the associate members, who agreed to adopt a common code of conduct regarding the management of quotas. This was achieved through the intervention of Alí Rodríguez, the Minister of Energy and Mines. The Venezuelan proposal was to create a band system of prices, which established a non-discretional rule for production, according to price movements, either above or below the band's ceiling and floor. That rule has worked well throughout this period, which was characterized by a notable price improvement, but it has already become obsolete as a consequence of the stratospheric prices that oil has reached since the United States' invasion of Iraq.

In 2000, within the context of his oil policy, Chávez hosted the first summit of the heads of state of OPEC in 25 years, in Caracas. The first summit took place in Algiers in 1975. This gap between summits reflects the cartel's difficulties in harmonizing the politics of its members. However, the summit was a success, which was recognized in Venezuela by both Tories and Trojans, perhaps because for us Venezuelans OPEC is part of our unconscious psychological heritage. To make sure of success the president had visited all members of the organization, but because Chávez did not exclude any of the members, there was outrage. In other words, Chávez had broken the old taboo imposed by the United States when he visited Iraq and Libya, two of the regimes the United States has on its "Index". So, in my opinion, Chávez proceeded correctly. If he, as the host, had acted discriminately towards some of the members, especially if the discrimination was not for reasons of national politics but owing to criteria established and imposed by the government of the United States, no contribution would have been made to the unity of OPEC or to the revival of its capacity for action. Venezuela is, in practice, an ally of the United States, but that does not mean that our foreign policy should be unconditionally aligned to that of America, or that we should love whomever they love and hate whomever they hate. Concerning the OPEC summit, it would have been almost incomprehensible if Chávez had visited representatives of some countries and left out others, especially if we consider that, by that time, the weakening of the Iraq embargo was becoming very visible, and that Libya was less subject to international pressure as a terrorist state after the trial of the perpetrators of the Lockerbie incident.

Where we cannot agree with Chávez is over the unnecessary, ridiculous and often absolutely ignorant effusiveness that he allows himself with some of the leaders of the Islamic countries. To visit Baghdad, Tripoli and Teheran is one thing, but it is quite another thing, and often quite ludicrous, to try to draw parallels between these countries' "revolutions" and that of Venezuela, even assuming that revolutions actually happened in these places, which in some instances is completely phantasmagoric. Apart from being members of OPEC, we have absolutely nothing in common politically with Saddam Hussein or Muammar Gadaffi, besides the fact that they are completely disgraceful characters. Very often these unnecessary gestures cause the objective being pursued to become distorted. Such behaviour only reinforces the impression of the general public, especially within our country, that his conduct is unnecessarily polemical, and this greatly irritates large swathes of Venezuelan public opinion.

Some of the opposition claim that Chávez has links with the terrorism that some of these countries have sponsored or are sponsoring; but this is totally irresponsible. To condemn Chávez's relationship with these countries, but with no supporting evidence, demonstrates either ignorance or deliberate deception, or both. Venezuela has maintained normal diplomatic relationships with the three countries mentioned since before the time of Chávez. These relationships have never previously been called into question in Venezuela, and especially not with the argument that they are "delinquent estates", as they are called in the rhetoric of the American State Department. Furthermore, Venezuela has not only unequivocally condemned the terrorist attacks against the United States, but just a few months previously, during the vote in Geneva for the UN Commission of Human Rights, Venezuela voted against sanctions against Cuba and China, but also, at the same time, abstained on the vote on Iraq, but no one in Venezuela seems to have noticed that.

As we have seen, some of the opposition's attitudes are too simplistic, extremely superficial, and deliberately deceptive. Their rule seems to be that when Chávez says "white" they must invariably say "black". There is a historical background to our relationships with the Islamic countries in general, and with the Arab countries in particular, which should not just be allowed to be sacrificed to the cause of circumstantial political interests.

Caracas, July 2003

## China: The cat's colour makes no difference

Deng Xiao Ping is generally regarded as the pragmatist *par excellence* ("what difference does the cat's colour make if it can still catch the mice"). Nevertheless, if the experiment that he started continues to be successful, it would not be surprising if in the future, when historical studies of the post-Mao period come to be written, we find out that not only was the man one of the greatest visionaries in history but that he was also a profound Marxist thinker. It was in the post-Mao period that China began to live with the effects of the ancient leader's proposals, which had been adopted at the core of the country's ruling Communist Party. To me, his way of doing things was not only pragmatic—which, ultimately, is not at all bad in small doses—but, above all, entailed the application of theoretical conceptualizations.

In 1917, it was the Mensheviks—who were going against the tide of Lenin's notion of "voluntarism"[25]—who correctly read Marx's text. They postulated the opening of a channel for capitalist development in the recently revolutionized empire as a necessary condition for the eventual advent of socialism. Marx had briefly touched on this issue in his memorable prologue to *A Critique of Political Economy*. No social regime yields its place in history to any other before completely exhausting the development of its productive forces. If we detach ourselves from general Marxist thinking, it can be argued that without prior and sufficient bases for production, which are absolutely necessary, it is impossible to build new relationships between production and property, and the mechanisms of economic "physiology". In other words, it is impossible to develop new relationships between property and production in a socialist society that is based on undeveloped, pre-capitalist methods of production, or in any society where capitalist development is in a precarious condition. A few years later, after the failure of the NPE (*Nueva Política Económica*, New Political Economy), Lenin again engaged with his master's fundamental position, in the sense of understanding the necessity of coordinating the revolutionary government with the private initiative of the wider economy. By the way, this strategy was successful in what, economically speaking, could be considered to be the first experience of a social democracy in history. It was unfortunately overturned by Stalin a few years later, when he re-nationalized the economy in the bloody exercise of the policy of voluntarism.

Mao Ze Dong, on his part, also believed that it was possible for China—a rural, feudal country in an awfully backward condition, to develop into a socialist state, purely though a strong will. "The Great Leap Forwards", as it was called, ended in colossal failure, as did the "Cultural Revolution" many years later, which was Mao's last effort to overcome the economic, social and political perversions generated by a totalitarian and ultra-left-wing society. From the chaos of the Cultural Revolution, with all the useless deaths and destruction, Deng Xiao Ping emerged as a far-reaching visionary.

---

[25] See footnote 24

His proposition was clear, profound, and had many consequences. China could only overcome its lack of development and the abysmal poverty of its enormous population by making use of the formidable potential of capitalism to expand the economy. It was then necessary to reconcile the government of the Communist Party, the dictatorship, and those at the political centre, to the idea of such an enormous change in the operation of the economy. Without doubt, this has constituted nothing but the re-establishment of capitalism in the commercial and service sectors and in certain areas of industry regions. The country has opened its economic borders to allow foreign investment in all sectors, in some instances as pure investment, in others through joint enterprises between the state and some of the most important trans-national companies in the world. In the countryside the communes have disappeared, and hundreds of millions of farmers now work their small holdings, which they manage themselves. The Chinese communists call this "market socialism", a euphemism to cover up the huge experiment of releasing the productive forces of capitalism on an underdeveloped China, but under strict control of the Communist Party. Deng probably reread those brilliant first few pages of the *Communist Manifesto*, in which Marx and Engels describe in epic terms the powerful, and at the same time contradictory, transformative power of early capitalism. Since it first began operating on a global scale, around the time when Columbus arrived in America, capitalism has contributed enormously to the process of human development. However, of course, a price has been paid for this, in the destruction of civilizations and entire cultures, and in the genocidal massacres and brutal social polarization that characterize developed capitalist countries. But Marx and Engels continued to reiterate the significance of the powerful drive for the development of productive forces in those societies, which implied the establishment of the relationships of capitalist production. The *Manifesto* states that:

> In the short century during which a new kind of upper class has existed, the bourgeoisie has created productive energies that are much larger and more grandiose than those of all past generations put together. It is enough to consider the role of machinery and the subjugation of natural forces by the hand of man, the application of chemistry to industry and agriculture, transport by steam-powered boats, the railways, the electronic telegraph, the mechanical ploughing of entire continents, the canals, the new towns that have sprung up miraculously from the dirt. In past centuries, who could have thought that in the lap of a society fertilized by the work of men we could find so much energy and so many kinds of production?

Having survived the ill-fated "cultural revolution", the aging Deng must have reflected philosophically whether or not the time had arrived for his country to use all the transformative power that Marx and Engel had described, the power of a capitalism that in the time of Marx and Engels was light years before the technical and economical marvels that now exist, and which make the "wonders" mentioned by the authors of the *Manifesto* look almost naïve in comparison.

Maybe Deng also remembered those brief lines by Marx in the prologue to the first volume of *Das Capital*. Marx stated that the destiny of underdeveloped countries was manifest in whatever was then happening in the capitalist countries that had already developed. They were the mirror that they should have looked at. Marx wrote in 1867 that "the industrially developed countries provide a mirror of the future for countries that are less developed". The Leninist concept of voluntarism—and possibly also Mao himself—discarded Marx's analysis of the situation. The aging Deng took a different approach; he realized that the old bearded patriarch of communism seemed to have had a better rationale than the revolutionaries of later generations, and he therefore acted accordingly. It does not matter what colour the cat is provided it catches the mice: China must develop itself to be able to feed its millions of inhabitants. If the capitalist cat can catch the mouse of under-development, then by all means, let it go ahead.

From a material point of view, the result of Deng's vision in China has simply been extraordinary. Beijing and Shanghai, especially the latter, are gleaming cities, and quite different to how they were when I saw them a quarter of a century ago. As in every great city, the streets and avenues are lined with all sorts of shops and businesses and studded with luxury malls (all the great western brands are there). Everything is privately owned. The privatization of China has reached enormous proportions, and from this process is emerging an extensive middle class and a small bourgeoisie, moreover a bourgeoisie whose millionaires can become members of the party. This is a party that no longer defines itself as one which only represents the peasants and working classes, but also as a party for China's capitalists. I asked my guides in Shanghai whether people are conscious of the new social contradictions that are becoming evident. There is now a middle class that will inevitably seek a place in the political limelight. There are now capitalists and labourers who produce capital that ends up in private hands. And, of course, my guides were aware of this. We spoke at length about what the Party's recent Congress had decided to do in that regard. Among the main worries for the party is how it will manage the new social and regional inequalities, which are now accentuated by the differences between the gleaming coastal cites and those that are further inland: while annual per capita income in Shanghai is $5000, in the countryside it is $300. I asked about political changes and the democratization of the rigorous political control exercised by the Communist Party. I got an allegoric answer: "The west has not clearly understood the enormous effect of the peaceful transition from Jiang Ze Ming to Ju Jintao regarding the direction of the party. Here, there are now no more "leaderships for life"; they now have fixed terms...We are liberalizing but we don't want to make the same mistakes that the Soviet Union made in its over-hasty opening-up of the political process". Democratization is indeed a long and slow process. It is one of humanity's recurrent issues. My guide said that "'History' will also understand Tiananmen Square". (When I use the term "History", I use a capital "H" when I refer to the history of a people with more than five thousand years of civilization behind them). In this new way of talking in China we cannot find anything of the stiff, stereotypical and dogmatic attitude that prevailed in previous times. A young functionary who accompanied me from Beijing differed from his Shanghai colleague. He was somewhat introverted, and timidly argued with my guide from Shanghai, but with me he lost all inhibitions. He told me that "the comrades in Shanghai live in an ivory tower", and I was able to witness, in these two people, an example of the play of the contradictions in China: it seems to indicate that in Shanghai they live at 78 RPM while in the rest of China they still revolve at 33 RPM.

The *China Daily* is an English-language newspaper, similar to the *Herald Tribune*, which even has the results of the Big League Games, obviously for the benefit of the millions of foreigners (most of whom are *gringos*) who frequent the big, hectic cities of China. I found an article in it, which strongly criticized the investment in Formula 1 car racing and a new race-course. I asked if the Chinese press is usually allowed to be so bold, and the answer was yes. "Can the head of government or their politics be criticized? No, that cannot be done". But this was immediately followed by an explanation: "but we will also become more liberal in this matter". But could this be just the "ivory-tower" liberality of the people of Shanghai? In any case, the notion that "we will also become more liberal in this matter" implies, no doubt, the typical rhythm of China. Their idea of time is very different to our own, as would naturally be the experience in a country that is thousands of years old. Therefore, when they speak of the future, a westerner should understand that this could mean dozens or even hundreds of years. None of the information media is private, and there is no concession in this matter. But television now has an enormous number of channels and is a world away from the single channel of the old Soviet countries. Mao would be turning in his grave (in the past, the visitor was obliged to visit it, but now it is not even suggested), if he were to know that you can now see a specialist on feminine beauty on a television program explaining how to enhance your bust.

China is now different, but it has been an uneven change, and we must be clear about this. Its rhythm, social life and territory are heavily controlled and managed by the state's Communist Party. There is a plan, and in the macro-economic sphere nothing has been completely liberated to the blind forces of the market. The state intervenes, although with uncommon flexibility. It decides everything, but, importantly, it does it without ignoring market signals. They have understood that no bureaucracy, as efficient as it may be—and it very rarely is—can operate as a substitute for the market in the process of distributing economic resources to society. In addition, in China, as noted previously, the notion of "time" is different. For us westerners, "time" is always hectic; in China things go more slowly and patiently. During a visit to a beautiful park in Shanghai that is said to be four hundred years old, I asked with surprise, considering the high level of maintenance, if it really was that old. My guide heartily laughed and said: "four hundred years is nothing". I remembered Mao's anecdote: once a member of the PCV asked Mao how long he thought the struggle with the USSR would last. Mao answered very seriously: "eight thousand years". The roots of this millenarian culture lie in the substrate of this alchemy, which is the "market of socialism". I was chatting with that same member of the Communist Party in Shanghai. I don't know whether or not he represented a new political mentality, but he was a lot more open and tolerant, and his erudition concerning Confucius,

Lao Tse and Buddhism—and the natural way in which he explained it—could make you think that he is not a unique case. "You are a 'Marxist-Leninist-Buddhist'" I said to him, in a joking manner. I don't think I could have got away with this twenty-five years ago, the first time I was there. Another unexpected surprise, which showed me how things are changing, was a visit to the Volkswagen factory, a joint venture between the Chinese state and the German company. This impeccable and fully automated factory has fifteen thousand workers. We had to wait about five or seven minutes at the front gates while a security guard verified our identity by phone. In previous times—as I said to my guide—a visitor arriving in the company of a party leader would not have gone through this ordeal. He agreed with me. "Before it would have been: "I am the boss, open the door"". *Eppur si muove.*

Some time ago, during the 1920s, a well-known American liberal, Lincoln Steffens, came back from the Soviet Union asserting that he had seen the future, "and it works", he concluded excitedly. As we know, he was enormously mistaken. It did not work and it collapsed—as Marx once thought was going to happen to capitalism—a victim of its own contradictions.

I do not know whether China is the future and whether it will work, but in any case it has shown an alternative to the tragic and frustrating experience of the Soviet Union. Its future still holds an unanswered question: what will be the outcome of the contradiction between their prodigious economic development, with the enhanced social mobility that follows it, and their political dictatorship? In today's China, in the middle of fierce capitalist growth, freedom is not a cardinal feature of their society. So, how could a political opening arise that would allow democracy to flourish in such a gigantic country, while at the same time also guaranteeing that the road to justice will be free?

Caracas, November 2004

# PART III

**Venezuela: The media and the political crisis**

In the relationship between the media and governments there are always moments of serious friction and even tempestuous clashes, even in countries where the relationship is relatively harmonious. Of course, I do not need to make the point that I am referring to countries with democratic governments, because in the case of oppressive regimes the problems are completely different. In democratic societies there exists a special "flexibility" in which media owners generally accommodate to the rules of the game imposed by authority, including censorship. But in a democracy the relationship between political power and the powers of the media is not always comfortable, especially in countries like ours, where the fragility of its institutions is proverbial. There is a dilemma between, on the one hand, freedom of expression, which is sustained by the media's status as private enterprise; and on the other hand, civil rights, which are expressed through the mechanisms of democratic electoral representation. Currently, we might not have simple, one-line answers to the question of how the inherent contradictions should be managed, but we cannot ignore the pertinence of this problem which, by the way, is not only ours in Latin-America, but is also of concern to the older and more stable western democracies. The contradictions between the power of the media and political power illustrate a real and universal problem: the necessity for political power to maintain a sufficient degree of autonomy from the media, in the face of the generally growing dominion of the great media powers and the partial interests that these represent, especially in electronic broadcasting.

The issue that has just been highlighted needs further exploration. The print and electronic media generally belong to powerful private companies and/or family groups, and in some instances to very powerful individual tycoons. It would be far too simplistic to conclude that the lines of information broadcast by the media are always dictated by their owners. If that were true across the board, then in all fields of information journalists would be nothing but simple puppets. However, there is no doubt that the socioeconomic, political and "existential" interests of the private sector are defended and voiced by their own media, regardless of the opinion of the journalists who work for them and whether or not such interests clash with those of the general population or the common good. In general, media owners place their particular interests above those of the country or the community. For this reason, within the world of privately owned media, or within any small or large privately owned enterprise, there is essentially no democracy; the "physiology" of such institutions is autocratic. The owner's will is never questioned or discussed. Furthermore, when governments resort to forms of censorship, either openly as in dictatorships, or in more sophisticated and subtle ways—especially through economic pressure, which is resorted to by some democratic governments—it is usually well known within any organization concerned, and it would be of general public interest both within the country and to the international media. But when media owners censor something, or veto or prohibit particular news or famous personalities from appearing, the issue scarcely goes beyond the walls of the newspaper offices or the radio and television studios. The SIP (*Sociedad Interamericana de Prensa*, Inter-American Press Association) is worried about threats to freedom of speech that are emanating from government, but it has never expressed even the most minimal disquiet in regards to the almost daily implementation of the internal censorship of the press. And in any case, it would not do it any good, because it would be like shooting yourself in the foot.

With the irruption of television and its subsequent transformation into the main means of mass communication, the power of the media and the interests that support it have now reached an influence and a capacity for public intervention never seen before, to the point that it has become common among communication theoreticians and academics to speak of "media-democracy" or "television-democracy" as a synonym for the ancient word "democracy". This poses a new set of problems for us, for which there are not any easy solutions. These problems cannot be bypassed by using the pretext of the defence of freedom of expression, when it is clear that in many cases this pretext is just an excuse for the protection of "not-so-general" interests. Television has become an invasive and omnipresent media, whose target is the individual and collective consciousness; in an ideal world, it could instead be a powerful tool for human development, assuming, of course, that this business, such as it is, would be able to escape the tyranny of ratings and uncontrollable greed, which impose a perverse and singular dynamic on the market. Privately-owned television is the only business where, as one of the ways to show competence in business, there doesn't need to be any improvement in product quality, but, on the contrary, competence is based on the strange paradox that the worse the product is, the greater the sales are, and therefore the greater the profit. This is at least empirically demonstrated in the history of global television, an example being the evident deterioration of the quality of television in some European countries after the ending of state monopolies, when private companies became established.

Private television networks usually compete to see who can fill the screen with the most vulgarity, violence and pornography. According to the media "philosophers", this is what people want and it produces the highest ratings. However, this is a specious argument that ignores the simple fact that the media's action itself constitutes or reinforces the viewers' tastes and preferences. Why any television network would want to introduce the worst kind of rubbish into their programming, such as *Laura in America*[26] for example, is an absolute mystery.

I believe it is indisputable that society has the right to protect itself against the effects of this kind of television. Though how this might be done is not easily answerable, because it transfers the debate to the very fragile terrain of freedom of expression. Up until now in Venezuela, even the television networks' own efforts have failed when trying to promote "codes of ethics". The state just adheres to the old and anachronistic rules of broadcasting, and has not gone any further in this area. For now, we are not going to pursue the general issue of the

---

[26] A "Jerry Springer" kind of show, hosted by a Peruvian doctor, Laura Bozzo.

content of broadcasting, which was just raised, but instead consider one of its crucial facets: the relationship between the media and the power of government, which, in a strict sense, is nothing else but the relationship between the media, especially television, and democracy. As has rightly been pointed out by the Venezuelan television researcher Fernando Rodríguez: "Even Popper, that great saint of liberal thought, recognized that without the proper regulation of television the proper functioning of democracy is doomed". And Rodríguez also goes on to say: "the argument is very simple; it only needs to be pointed out that if just a few people have a monopoly over the voices that the public hear, then real debate in the public arena becomes unviable". Venezuela, from the time before Chávez as well as during his government, provides a useful and illustrative case study in this respect, because it is precisely in a democracy that this issue acquires particular relevance.

Before Chávez's accession to power, in the period when the post-Pérez Jiménez democratic governments ruled the country, it was really only during Carlos Andrés Pérez's second government, from 1989 to 1993 (he was removed from government in 1993), that the relationship between the media and the government became what could be described as traumatic. During Luis Herrera Campins' Social-Christian government, there were strong frictions between the media (especially the television networks) and the government, but they did not reach the levels of confrontation that they had reached during the time of Pérez's government, in particular with the daily newspaper *El Nacional*. In general, a sort of "normality" ruled the country at that time, basically determined by a *modus vivendi* that had been reached between the leading political parties (AD and Copei) and the media. This was sustained by a sort of non-written agreement, by which the government allowed the media to make a lot of money with poor quality broadcasts with little cultural content, which were not subject to any regulation. The media, particularly television, essentially reinforced the polarity between AD and Copei inherent in the balance of national political forces, which prevented the expression of any new political alternative. By maintaining a kind of "neutral" position, the media became essentially "apolitical", abstaining from any real political expression. (I should add that the only time this silence was broken was during Carlos Andrés Pérez's government.) The situation became so extreme that the main newspapers in the country had their own parliamentary groups, comprising media employees, only some of whom were journalists, who gained access to Congress through the parliamentary boards of different political parties.

On one occasion, in 1988, while I was a presidential candidate for MAS—which meant being excluded from the previously mentioned pact between the government and the media—I received a call from one of the most powerful media bosses in the country. He told me that one of his employees was already a candidate of AD for parliament, that another was with Copei, and that he wanted to also put one on our board. My loud, angry and negative response was followed by a threat: "then you'll have to deal with the consequences". Those "consequences" meant a brutal campaign during the last two months of the run-up to the elections, when I was daily presented as the perpetrator of all the killings that happened during the years of armed struggle in Venezuela during the 1960s. Numerous articles appeared on the various incidents of that confrontation, which were accompanied by a profusion of macabre photographs, even though the country had already politically overcome those events in an exemplary process of reconciliation. However, there is no doubt that the effect of that campaign was very detrimental to MAS and myself, its presidential candidate. But this interference in the political process nevertheless went unpunished, and the aberrant "rights" that the large media groups had acquired were never curtailed nor even questioned by any of the main, traditional Venezuelan political parties; quite the opposite, they were paying the price for access to television and the print media, hoping to preserve a privileged relationship in view of the future elections. This perversion of the democratic process was tolerated, almost unbelievably, as not only the political parties but, worse still, also the state and the government abdicated from their normal political roles. As had been demonstrated in the past, such conduct was suicidal for Venezuelan politicians as well as their parties.

However, in the case of the television media there was an exception to the distortion of the political process. As previously mentioned, President Luis Herrera Campins (1979–1984) had created a controversy by railing against some of the unusual attacks on him by some of the television networks, the consequence being that political influence triumphed over the world of the media. In addition, Herrera Campins' government banned advertisements for alcohol on television, limited soap operas to sixty episodes, proposed the obligatory scheduling of cultural programs on prime-time television (which, by the way, has never been respected), as well as the protection of children's usual viewing times. However, these decisions never really amounted to more than "Platonic" regulations, which the television networks successfully opposed, and were never implemented (with the sole exception of alcohol advertisements). Though, as a result—in a kind of dreadful revenge—Herrera Campins has been effectively banished from some of the television networks until now, in a sort of perpetual veto.

A second important incident happened shortly after the coup led by Hugo Chávez on the 4th of February 1992. In an act of contrition, the leading parties designated a Commission for Constitutional Reform, presided over by Rafael Caldera, who was then a senator. This commission developed a project, which had first been discussed in parliament, for the reform of the *Magna Carta*.[27] When, during discussions, they reached the article on freedom of expression, the concepts of "truthful information" and "the right to reply" unleashed the fury of the media, and a savage campaign ensued "in the defence of freedom of expression". This campaign vilified the previously mentioned article, and the media rudely manipulated public opinion through crude, mendacious television adverts. The parliament, which was controlled by the traditional political parties, not only shelved the article but the entire project as well. Although the national mood was ripe for constitutional reform, it did not happen. It is worth noting that a

---

[27] Venezuela's constitution.

few years later Hugo Chávez, through the *Constituyente* (the reform of the constitution), used constitutional reform to gain votes during his 1998 electoral campaign. Ironically, in the run-up to the elections it was the media that helped create the conditions that led to Chávez arriving in power. Coincidentally, at that time when neo-liberal thought, particularly concerning politics, was flourishing in the country, it was being proclaimed that all the misfortunes that our nations have to endure had been caused by the state. The television networks abandoned their previous "apolitical approach" and assumed the role of protagonist regarding the future direction of the nation. As we have now seen, their actions completely boomeranged, resulting in the coming to power of Commander Chávez, who was an unexpected manifestation of "anti-politics". The media subsequently discovered that he was the kind of contender who had not been dreamed of even in their worst nightmares.

Chávez reaped the results of a fifteen-year-long media campaign aimed at the destruction of the political parties and the demonizing of politics and politicians, though the traditional parties were also largely responsible for the long crisis that resulted in the great turnaround that produced Chávez's victory. The parties contributed enormously to their own suicide, but it is also true that for decades they were the victims of a sustained and systematic campaign that was undertaken from a neo-liberal perspective of the need to minimise the role of state, and which swept the floor from under the politicians, political parties and politics in general. They were all demonized as inefficient and corrupt by definition, and all in the name of a supposedly efficient and morally unblemished spirit of free enterprise. It used to be said that the time of the "politicians" had ended, and that it was the beginning of the time of the "managers". It was pointed out by Fernando Rodríguez, who was mentioned previously, that "politics has become too serious to leave in the hands of the politicians. And the media was on hand to accomplish the mission of demolishing the omnipotent state and its clerics, all of whom congregated into parties that had been very damaged since the infamous "black Friday", when we all ceased to be 'rich Saudis'". The politicians' responsibilities—which were not insignificant—and their own guilt, together with a persistent trend in the country towards an "anti-political" ideology, opened the gates wide for the Commander, Hugo Rafael Chávez Frías. He made a triumphal entrance, enveloped in the halo of bravado that always seems to crown men of action in our continent; he was the avenger of all evils and wrongdoings caused by politicians, the anti-politician *par excellence*, the perfect outsider, someone who didn't compromise with the disgraceful party democracy of the past. Here was someone who the majority of the population saw as the embodiment of the rejection of party democracy—which later caused great consternation among those who adopted it—of politicians' perversions, corrupt behaviour and abuses of power, some of which were real, some of which were false, and some of which were greatly exaggerated.

Of course it would be an exaggeration to consider the media as being completely responsible for the political upheaval that resulted in the emergence and success of the Chávez cult. In reality, they were just part of the cast, important actors but not the only ones; they were part of a process during which, over almost two decades, the decadence of the "AD-Copei republic" extended, and when economic, social and political components began to inextricably entwine. Nevertheless, from a non-democratic and far right perspective, the media's role in the deconstruction of this monopoly cannot be underestimated, because ultimately they were not just "mirrors" of the crisis. Although this is how they usually and indulgently describe themselves, they were, however, central players in the game, and politically belligerent. As was perfectly described by a powerful media boss: "they could install or remove governments". Only really during the crisis that culminated in the departure of Carlos Andrés Pérez can it be said with propriety that there was a real crisis in the management of government, which, incidentally, was largely due to the involvement of the media. We cannot ignore the fact that for many years the media went beyond reliable criticism of government and entered an arena of vitriolic offensive against the democratic system and, *tout court*, democracy itself, which greatly contributed to Chávez's access to power. In fact, some within the media considered this to be their own victory. As was pointed out by the ex-president Caldera a few months ago, what the media never imagined would happen was that they were not going to be able to bribe or co-opt him.

During the time of Chávez's government, the already very tense relationship between the media and political powers has reached a climax. This is not any more about mere "tensions" but instead has turned into an open and callous confrontation, which almost six years later seems to be coming to an end, with a clear victory for Chávez. Unfortunately, this is not a victory for democratic society, but for authoritarianism, personal rivalries and the autocratic management of power, which now, ironically, also demonizes the media, in the same way that happened in the past with politics and even democracy. With the yielding of the media, Chávez has seen the creation of new kinds of relationships between power and the media, but on a non-democratic platform, which threatens freedom of expression, and which also allows the reinforcement of an authoritarian and autocratic form of government. Just consider how the cure could end up being worse than the illness, if, as we can foresee, everything ultimately culminates in laws that "sensibly" reduce the room for freedom of expression. This could possibly happen with the Law of Social Responsibility in Radio and Television, which is about to be approved by the National Assembly. This new law contains reforms to the Penal Code that could criminalize particular forms of political action and journalistic expression.

Maybe it would be good to remember how all of this started in Venezuela. During the 1998 elections, Chávez was treated generously by the newspapers and the audio-visual media. As soon as it became obvious that his candidacy was becoming stronger, the media opened up to him and his performance was then widely covered. In fact, we could talk of a sort of "alliance" between Chávez and the main daily paper in Caracas, as well as with the main national television network. After his election as president, Chávez's appointment of the Prime Minister to the Secretariat was Alfredo Peña, the ex-director of *El Nacional*, and the person appointed as the Minister of Information was none other than the wife of the owner of that newspaper. This should indicate to the reader just how cordial the relationship was between the media and the new president, though it must be said that at least during the first year of his mandate this relationship was generally correct.

But incessant problems began to arise. Chávez became annoyed with information that he considered to be inaccurate, and with the criticism of his management of the government. He turned from refutation and reasoned protest and went on the offensive, which was often brutal and intolerant towards the owners of newspapers and television networks. Not much time passed before the media acquired a similar tone in their responses to him, and worse, some of the media bosses adopted stances that undoubtedly encouraged a climate of conspiracy and anti-democracy. The first sign of this was the rebellion in April 2002, in the *coup d'état* that resulted in the overthrow of the president for a few hours. Then, in October 2002, we witnessed the insurgency of hundreds of military officials, who subsequently occupied Altamira Square in Caracas for a year. Between December 2002 and January 2003 we had a prolonged and senseless "civic" strike that lasted for two months. Until now the owners of the media have avoided discussing the issue of their responsibility for the events; and there are no significant signs on either their part or that of the government of any sense of critical reflection.

Could events have been turned out otherwise? To speculate in this way is always a useless exercise, but it is worth considering how we ended up in the irrational clashes that we have had to endure almost since the beginning of this government. On the one hand, the authoritarian and autocratic tendencies of our president, combined with his immaturity and inexperience, have caused him to manage his relationship with the media in a clumsy way. He is always attacking them with completely undiplomatic immoderation and making crass generalizations about them and their owners. On the other hand, the arrogance of those with actual power, as much in the media as in the economic sphere, derived from always being used to the eventual submission of politicians. Those who had actual power in these arenas believed they could apply the same formula against Chávez, as in the past they had successfully confronted political power.

However, President Chávez confronted the media with a strategy that employed a kind of opaque and absurd reductionism, denouncing them as the incarnation of "the oligarchy" and promoting a climate of physical aggression towards journalists and the media. For their part, people with power in the media and the economy embarked on a course of political rebellion. But their point of departure was based on a completely wrong diagnosis of the nature of Chávez's government, which they defined in absurdly simplistic terms, as "dictatorial" and "totalitarian". (And, it must be said, the president did not help by unnecessarily aggravating the situation with his provocative behaviour and incendiary rhetoric.) This became increasingly apparent in the way in which the media managed information, opinion, and television programming, which were all manipulated according to the idea of a so-called "fast-track solution" for our political crisis.

You could say there was a clash between two types fundamentalism. On one side there was a right-wing fundamentalism, which looked at itself as the incarnation of "freedom": any action of the government that did not correspond to their conception of the world was described as an attack or as a threat; and they also always confused their own economic interests and social privileges with the interest of the country as a whole. On the other side was classic left-wing fundamentalism, which was imbued with its typical, characteristic teleology of the evolution of humanity: they see themselves as the incarnation of "Truth, Justice and History", and any political disagreement with them was considered to be a threat or an attack on an overarching "meta-political" ideology. Both kinds of fundamentalism, in their worst forms of expression, have served as ideological supports that have underpinned terrible dictatorships and horrendous totalitarian governments in the twentieth century. It was during the long-gone times of the French revolution when Saint Just coined the terrible maxim: "The revolution must be defended in its entirety; anyone who discusses its details betrays it". In the case of the left wing, this could be considered as the motto of all the Stalinist governments that have existed in the past and of those that are waiting to emerge. Revolutionary mentality is absolutely intransigent: within the revolution everything is valid, but outside it nothing at all. This was once strongly asserted by Fidel Castro but in slightly different terms: "if you are not with the revolution then you are against it". In other words, any opposition is "counter-revolutionary" by definition, and it cannot be tolerated. It is well known that in revolutionary dictatorships the "rebels" are generally shot or they are sentenced to extremely long terms in jail, and are very rarely pardoned under an amnesty. Chávez has resigned himself to verbally "shooting" the paradoxical counter-revolution that he himself created, especially through his intimidating rhetoric, and in a country where there has not been any real "revolution", whatever meaning you give to the word. As one of Chávez's main collaborators (now in the opposition) once said: "Chávez has misled half of the country with a non-existent revolution, and has frightened the other half with the threat of it.

Chávez came to power despite the political and social rejection of him by forty percent of the country, who are a lot more apprehensive of the strong language he uses against the old political establishment, rather than of his supposedly "revolutionary" method, which was not explicit at all during the election campaign. Nonetheless, rather than trying to neutralize his adversaries, his rather delirious viewpoint—which was full of the type of immature ultra-leftist thinking that was so strongly criticized by Lenin—simply ended up as interminable verbal diarrhoea, replete with the topics typical of the Bourbon left. It consequently transpired that what had begun as just a simple vote "against him", first transformed into mistrust and then into fear. His threatening speeches, his other-worldly eulogies to the Cuban regime (with which he later developed a sort of "carnal relationship"), his misguided attitude during the first eighteen months of his government towards the Colombian guerrillas (which he later corrected, but after the damage had already been done), his brutal rhetoric against his adversaries, and the absolutely anti-democratic and authoritarian way in which he presented the famous "decree laws" at the end of 2001, altogether resulted in completely scaring the middle and upper classes. They were led to fear a future influx of *balseros* (Cuban boat people), which aroused a sense of concern among vast swathes of the public, who consequently accepted a non-democratic strategy of struggle in confronting the phenomenon with which they had been presented. Some of those in opposition—especially on a social level—adopted a stance of counter-revolution. However, their position was as ideological as that of the president, and the "revolution" that they were confronting was in essence a fabrication: the situation was Kafkaesque. Not only was there no evidence of anything revolutionary but you could not even talk of any progressive reforms, beyond, of course, the social programs that Chávez baptised as "missions", which, ultimately, are neither reforms nor are they revolutionary. There has been a great deal of self-styled "revolutionary" verbiage, which is really just "noise and fury". However, this has had a devastating effect on the general mood of Venezuelans, and has split the country into two halves, which is illustrated in recent results from elections. The ultra-left politics of Chávez is the kind of politics that has caused so much damage in other Latin American countries undergoing processes of social change.

As a consequence of Chávez's victory in 1998, the system of political parties collapsed In Venezuela. Since we were effectively lacking political parties, the tide of opposition, which was initially diffuse and unorganized, and which later became increasingly widespread and combative, started to seek refuge in the media. The media, which are, of course, deeply linked to economical, social and political interests, not only welcomed the tide of opposition, with which, naturally, they had a great empathy, but also contributed to the strengthening of the movement. Eventually they became part of it, in addition providing the opposition with a direct conduit to the general public. During all of 2002, when the political parties were extremely weak, part of the media, in conjunction with the country's other effective powers, the economic and the military, assumed the same stance as that of the opposition. The media were the principal players in the events that took place on the 11th of April, as well as in the insurrection by a group of military officials on October the 10th. These same officials later took over Altamira Square for a whole year, where they staged a continuous "show" of rebellion, which was generously disseminated by the media, especially on television. The media were also instrumental in the two-month-long strike that took place from December 2002 to January 2003.

The implacable dialectic of the confrontation has dragged down both the government and the media. Chávez manipulates the media; and he has lied; but the media have also lied; and both Chávez and the media distort the facts. And the truth of it is that both the government and the media have contributed to the breakdown of proper government. But to finish these lines on a note of precarious optimism, I would say that in the extraordinary laboratory of politics and the media that Venezuela has become in recent years, in a climate of asphyxiation—and in a struggle that has few comparisons—the majority of Venezuelans now share in a belief in a common criterion: that in a more sensible tomorrow we should develop ways and means of communicating that are not authoritarian or primitive, such as those of Chávez, and which do not have the arrogant style of the privately-owned, uncultured "tabloid" media. We could look to the wise, joint arrangements of some European countries, where there is a strong system deriving from the state and not from the government, where the state is economically solid and capable of using the best national talent, and of coexisting with the private sector, which is properly subject to ethical and targeted regulation. This kind of arrangement would allow us to reach a subtle balance between information and opinion, and would allow the enormous machinery of power to be turned towards education and culture. Although it is not necessary to demean entertainment or sport, nevertheless, we should not allow ourselves to be carried away by the multi-tentacled American television industry. In conclusion, society should be a real distillery of lucid and sensible citizens, who are open to dialogue and who understand that the game of institutions is the only way to make and remake collective life, and that they guarantee the curious concept that we call governance. To me, this is but another way of articulating peace and creative communication between people. Democracy, authentic democracy: let's hope we will get there some day.

Caracas, October 2004

## With our feet on the ground

Could Chávez have really won the RR (*Referéndo Revocatorio*, Recall Referendum)[28] on 15th April 2004? Here lies a disturbing but pertinent question, because a great deal of the opposition's behaviour after the referendum has been decisively based on the negative answer to that question: no. It is impossible that he won. Amongst the opposition it is said that his victory can only be explained as the culmination of a massive fraud, which produced an identical result, 60:40, but in favour of "yes". Moreover, the relative retreat of the opposition in the face of the obscene advantage that characterised Chávez's ultimately victorious campaign, and the shameless dilatory manoeuvres and the trickery of a majority of government representatives within the National Electoral Council (CNE), all seem to be symptomatic of the same triumphalist mentality: "it doesn't matter, because the avalanche of the 'yes' votes will annul the effects of all the cheating". As a consequence, the outcry against the cheating has been subdued. Everything had been entrusted in the impossibility of losing. Worse still—if we consider the serious consequences that this could produce—the confidence in their ultimate victory was such that the high command of the opposition had not even contemplated any strategy with which they would be able to respond in the event of a victory by Chávez. However, on his part, Chávez is said to have had a "plan B" in case of defeat. ("If I lose I will hand over to José Vicente Rangel and I'll get ready for the next campaign".) Such a state of affairs explains why Carrasquero's pre-emptive action caught the opposition totally unprepared and politically unarmed.

Among the opposition, there was confidence in victory; an exaggerated optimism had been fomented by the exit polls, which had been carried out by organizations such as "Súmate". But on the other hand, there was the tempestuous and absolutely abnormal way in which the "no" victory was prematurely announced. In my opinion, this drove the CD (*Coordinación Democrática*) to react over-hastily in denouncing a fraud that they claimed had been committed during the election process. However, at the time, what was lacking was even the slightest material evidence of fraud.

So, was it really impossible that Chávez actually won? We can now confront this question with the calmness and coolness that perhaps would not have been possible during the early morning of April the 16th. Before the referendum there were sufficient signs that his victory was not improbable. Let's look at the most significant aspects.

1. All the polls had predicted the "no" vote as the winner. Only one, from the UCV (*Universidad Central de Venezuela*) had registered a different result, but the deficiencies and defects of this poll were so obvious that even an idiot could

---

[28] The Recall Referendum is a mechanism that was enshrined in a new Constitution, which was instituted by Chávez, whereby the people can call for a vote of confidence in the President in the middle of his or her term; this particular referendum was a vote of confidence in the government of Chávez.

detect them. Two weeks before the RR, Edmond Saade from "Datos" (Data) had confided to a small group of us that their survey had recorded a thirteen point lead for the "no" vote. A week before the RR, IVAD (*Instituto Venezolano de Análisis de Datos*), belonging to Felix Seijas, recorded an eleven-point lead for the "no" vote. Two other analysts' surveys, those of "Datanalisis" and "Consultores 21", had also indicated that the "no" vote would win. It is also worth considering that the last poll from "Consultores 21", made on the 13th of August in nine different cities, recorded the "no" vote at 52.9% and the "yes" vote at 47%; then compare these figures with the official result of the elections in those same nine cities: "no", 53%; "yes", 46.9%.

If these data were known to the CD (and there is no reason to doubt it because the information was practically in the public domain, and "Consultores 21" was working for the CD itself), why was more attention not paid to this information? I don't have a good answer for this. I would just like to mention a minor event, without going into too many details, as an indication of the triumphalist political climate of which we have spoken. I am talking about the fact that after Saade (from "Datos") had finished his remarks about the thirteen point lead for the "no'" vote, one of the directors from the CD who was among our small group told me quietly: "Don't pay any attention. 'Datos' is no more what it used to be and we have a poll from the UCV that shows a significant lead for the 'yes' vote". I must say I was left speechless by this absolutely surreal revelation.

2. Chávez's election campaign was conducted from a position of power, with all the advantages that a president in his position enjoys. It was conducted in a systematic violation of the most fundamental republican and democratic principles, which were without doubt curtailed. Chávez shamelessly took advantage of the situation, but without being subject to any kind of punishment. However, this shocking state of affairs cannot obscure something equally shocking but quite transparent: the contrast between the vigorous campaign in favour of "no" and the mediocre campaign of Chávez. The difference was so apparent that you could not help but notice it. The significant point is that the "yes" campaign did nothing in the west of Caracas or in any of the poorer quarters in other areas of the city (which was a phenomenon that was repeated in other major cities of the country). This clearly demonstrated the lack of inspiration and effectiveness of the "yes" campaign. Chávez, who, as mentioned previously, is known to have had a "plan B" in case there were any objections, implemented it the same night that he began to realize that there could indeed be objections. Instead of wasting time with challenges and other diversions, he organized a "show" during which he launched his political campaign, which he called "The Battle of Santa Inéz".[29] He also gave the entire Ayacucho Command[30] a roasting[31] and three days later organized the *"Maisanta"*.[32] While

[29] This was one of the most important battles in the history of Venezuela's independence, fought on 10th December 1859, in which the Federalists, led by General Ezequiel Zamora, were victorious.

[30] The Ayacucho Comando was a coordinating committee of political leaders of all parties that supported Chávez's government.

the CD argued for over two weeks about the arrangements for the command of its campaign, Chávez had already unfolded his campaign, which was, in addition, generously financed by public funds; and, as shamelessly announced by José Vicente Rangel, it used "the weight of the state" against Chávez's adversaries.

3. The CD did not manage to mount a successful challenge to the leadership of Chávez, not because they did not want to or could not, but because that was the reality of the situation. They were only able to present a diffuse, dispersed, contradictory, inevitable, and sluggish "Fourth-Republic"[33] cast of leaders. The uncertainty and distrust that was aroused in many of Chávez's opponents regarding the opposition's leadership also extended to a vision of the characteristics of the government that could have potentially displaced Chávez. Even if we find it difficult to admit, fears arose that in actually winning there would be the prospect of a weak government, which, in addition, could be quickly undermined by the differences between the various members of the CD. Most importantly, there was the consequent uncertainty on another level: who could be the next president after Chávez? Fears and uncertainties became heightened with the expectation of a conflict—even bigger than the current one—between a fragile government and an opposition lead by Chávez that would still be in control of the National Assembly and the other levers of power. Given that this very real scenario was unfolding during the run-up to the elections, could we perhaps reasonably infer that a not insignificant number of those in opposition, who could have voted against the president, decided to settle the score with Chávez at another time, in the elections of 2006, preferring to abstain or even—and there is evidence that this happened—to vote "no" instead?

4. Finally, we have the effect of the "missions". Here is not the place to discuss the concepts behind them or their relative worth. What matters is to point out how they might be affecting the more vulnerable in the population. Accustomed, as all Venezuelans are, to the populist practice of living off the income from the oil that finances the state, we can imagine the effect that the massive distribution of public funds through the different "missions" is producing, which, in addition, are accompanied by political rhetoric that has a resonance of social redemption among the people (as Chávez said: "Finally the profits from oil are reaching the people"). Furthermore, the polls have registered this point, which most likely did not go unnoticed by the directors of the CD. The "missions" have had the effect of reinforcing emotional and affective ties between Chávez and his followers, and also helped to bring back into the fold those who had become disenchanted. The "missions" cause many people to believe that there is a government that is thinking of the poor, which has them as a priority on its

---

[31] This was because of what was perceived as their gross incompetence: they had failed to collect enough signatures in support of Chávez.

[32] The *Maisanta* is a database that records the details and voting preferences of all Venezuelans on the electoral register. The name most probably derives from the name of the rebel Pedro Pérez Delgado, better known as Comando Maisanta (d. 1922), who was behind an uprising that resulted in the death of a Venezuelan ex-president and a state governor.

[33] Chávez refers to his political project as the Fifth Republic, while those he deems more "backwards" are said to belong to the Fourth Republic.

political agenda. In the midst of neglect and poverty, the perception that the attention of the president can be counted on is undoubtedly a powerful factor in his quest to maintain power. It is irrelevant to discuss this issue from the angle of Chávez's intentions. Whatever they may be—sincere or demagogic and manipulative, and most probably a combination of both—the important point is how the "missions" are perceived by the beneficiaries: there is a perception that if Chávez leaves, the poor would disappear from the agenda and the chequebook of the succeeding government. Chávez's rhetoric, together with the "missions", gives a sense of identity and belonging to the socially excluded. "With Chávez, it is not the case that 'we rule', but at least we count". Therefore, the electoral impact of the "missions" was predictable, which, as I mentioned previously, registered in the polls.

These indicators were sufficient to allow us to conclude that a victory by Chávez was not out of the question. However, before prematurely accusing Chávez of "fraud", it would perhaps have been advisable to adopt a more judicious attitude: it would have been wise to wait for the verdict of the international observers, who had been installed to guarantee the validity of the results. However, the CD directorate's attitude on that Monday morning of the 16th April conveyed—and reinforced—the initial reaction of a good part of the opposition's social base, who ended up feeling as though they been the victims of a robbery.

So, the reaction of those who voted "yes" is, in a way, understandable. For the voters on the 15th April, the certainty of having won was boosted by two factors. First, when the private television networks mostly transmitted images of the long electoral queues in the middle-class areas, the broadcasts helped to create the impression that it was mostly in these areas that there was enthusiasm for the elections. Many people did not even consider the possibility that on the other side of the city there were also queues, even larger, of people also waiting for many hours to vote "no". The failure to recognize the "other", so characteristic of both sides in this polarization that is tearing us apart, is expressed, even today, in the difficulty of admitting that the city and the country are a lot bigger than the particular street or the neighbourhood where we happen to live. The "other" simply does not exist. The second factor was the famous publication of the exit polls by Súmate. Even nowadays people still speak of them as if they were the Ten Commandments of Moses, and as though they were the only polls that took place that day. But the truth is that there were several exit polls, and I had the opportunity to see those which, logically, the government was conducting, as well as those from other independent sources, whose results were, of course, opposite to those of Súmate. Many people swear by the Súmate polls and argue that they are irrefutable and that there is no valid political argument against them. Therefore, when the official results became public people reacted with absolute scepticism. Nonetheless, as we found out later, Súmate's exit polls had serious technical irregularities; it is now impossible to continue to hold them up as evidence of a "yes" victory.

But on the other hand, what is not equally understandable is the identical reaction by the CD directorate. As has been already pointed out, in the CD were people who could have encouraged them to behave more judiciously, and not allowed them to continue spilling water that later could not be recovered.

On the morning of the 16th April, when the CD decided to denounce the "fraud", still without any proof in their hands, they fell prey of their own trap, attempting the impossible mission of squaring a circle: denouncing the fraud and yet also calling for votes in the forthcoming regional elections. However, the CD severely limited their possibilities for political action when they failed to respond immediately to the invitation to engage in a dialogue that had been astutely requested by Chávez. They decided to categorically and unanimously challenge the legitimacy of his victory, thereby cutting themselves off from the possibility of challenging Chávez on the same platform, to which they had been invited. If they had sought to improve the political—and even electoral—climate in the country, they could at least have temporarily occupied the same political territory. Moreover, they could have put to the test the real character of such an invitation to a dialogue. Only against an irrefutable proof of fraud is it possible to abdicate from political dialogue; and that was not the situation. Chávez was in a comfortable position, having won, and the certainty that he was going to remain in power; he had been able to foresee the election result clearly. Chávez also understood that he needed to build bridges with the other half of the country (which accounts for a great number of people) who oppose him. This is where an important part of the most organized political opinion is concentrated, and also where we find the majority of the technical, scientific, cultural and intellectual enterprises, as well as businesses of all sizes, the middle class, and part of the organized working class. When the CD dismissed the call to "dialogue" so quickly, and later proposed "conditions" to Chávez (which were completely impossible, by the way), they allowed Chávez to look like a speaker with stature, while the CD, on the contrary, looked narrow and sectarian; they thus gave ground to Chávez, who promptly resumed his customary quarrelsome style.

But even worse than that, such resistance to immediate political dialogue gravely jeopardized the CD's possibilities for action in the short term. With the regional elections being imminent, maintaining an unverified accusation of fraud within their policy would inevitably lead to a massive abstention by the opposition's voters. (In this regard it is perhaps relevant to mention that when someone is down, that's when "you put the boot in".) To ask the voters to disregard the allegations of fraud and then go to vote (which is what the opposition leaders are asking us to do) could have been seen by voters as an act of cynicism. It is difficult to denounce a fraud and to simultaneously ask for votes. The situation was further aggravated by the situation that as the accusation was not proven, it became very difficult to start a dialogue with the CNE (*Consejo Nacional Electoral,* National Electoral Council) in order to attend to the manifest irregularities that occurred during the RR and throughout the entire, long process. So, for now, the CD is losing out on two counts: losing their partisans, and in seeking a level playing field for the next election. The result is foreseeable: the opposition will probably lose the seats that they currently hold in some of the local councils and provincial governments, without winning any additional ones, which is something that would have been possible. Now we run the risk of giving

Chávez what is without doubt very significant power: the entire political and territorial administrative structure could end up in his hands, which could considerably reinforce his autocratic and authoritarian tendencies.

Becoming bogged down in the fraud issue could also create an extremely dangerous dynamic. If they are consistent, and if the CD's message continues to be the same, then they should end up calling on people to abstain from voting; that is, if they want to maintain a minimum of coherence. But at the same time, this is to go down a road that also has logical consequences; it would result in even more kindling being added to the fire of the more extreme and reckless elements of the party. (Incidentally, their policies are so impractical and unworkable that they would only end up creating new and worse setbacks.) In addition, going down that road would result in international isolation and the loss of the good will that the CD has gained around the world. However, as a consequence of the stance that they took in front of the international observers, the CD now looks severely damaged. The positions that the CD has adopted on various issues have caused a lot of perplexity abroad because they seem to be inconsistent. It is now not easy to try to convince the world that the true results from the RR were a 60:40 victory by the opposition.

The truth is that to start to have effective politics we must swallow hard and accept the facts; we have to plant our feet firmly on the ground. We had the RR, and the opposition took part in it. We have to accept the more or less obvious irregularities that characterized the process that started on the 19th of August 2003 and ended on the 15th of August of 2004. We also have to accept the obscene advantage that Chávez had during his campaign (with the argument that the avalanche of "yes" votes would annul the effects of their cheating); the result was endorsed by the OEA (*Organización de Estados Americanos*) and the Carter Center (and the CD had said that only an endorsement by organizations such as these would allow them to recognize the results); and subsequently numerous governments also recognized Chávez's victory. There is also an even more important fact: half of the country is sure that Chávez won. To ignore this (particularly considering the spiced-up conspiracy theories that emerged to explain the absence of "celebrations" on the winner's side) could be construed as another manifestation of the aforementioned tendency of some of those within the opposition to ignore the "other" even as a social group, which will only result in further deepening the abyss that separates the two halves of the country. In these conditions—and if we look beyond the discussions between mathematicians, statisticians and experts on the theory of relativity—the political reality for half the country and for the international community is that Chávez did not loose the RR. The results are politically valid, as are the great number of "yes" votes and the numerous seats that Chávez won. This is true even where there was in fact a "no" vote, where in principle it would have been perfectly possible to defeat *Chávismo* in a confrontation where local factors would have had a significant influence.

Only when we have moved on from this clash with reality will we be able to begin to formulate viable, democratic, long-term political strategies, because the political reality is that Chávez has over two more years in power, and it is in the light of this inescapable fact that the next steps must be taken. This entails, above all, the need to define a permanent structure within which the processes of government should operate, and not—as has been the case until now—only concentrating on the president's character. To exercise real opposition is something more than just exclaiming "Chávez must go". It involves a critical attitude to what the government does or does not do in its administration. In this regard we should remember that the opposition began to gain weight at the moment when it confronted the project on Education Law. The country needs to see opposition leaders speaking of something else besides Chávez. The whole process of government must be submitted to permanent, critical scrutiny by its adversaries. Confronting Chávez's selfishness, tyranny and authoritarianism does not mean that we should avoid analysing specific features of his administration. Demonstrating his "hold" over the general population also entails bringing to light the flaws of his administration in practical matters, ranging from his economic policy to social security and everything else in between. There is now room for the opposition's criticism, an opposition which has up until now been reduced to merely clashing with Chávez "the dictator", leaving little to enthuse the impoverished masses. Incidentally, this situation necessitates using not only the parliamentary benches but also the situations of popular struggle in the poor quarters, factories and the streets. Concerning parliamentary representation, many people think that the opposition has no more than forty delegates, who face eighty-six pro-government delegates, because debates always conclude with that number of people who vote; in fact the opposition has seventy-seven deputies. Maybe we should also ask ourselves whether the CD has now fulfilled a historical phase and whether this makes it necessary to consider some kind of more practical and flexible formula for the articulation of the opposition's political forces, while admitting the possibility of different centres of opinion and action. Such a reconstruction could provide those political parties which have a greater degree of autonomy to act, the possibility to further develop; it could hasten their reconstruction and also open a space for the emergence of other options.

But the essential issue is to define the kind of politics in the name in which action can be taken; and the starting point cannot be other than acceptance of the aforementioned fact of life: that Chávez will lead the country for at least two more years. This compels us to re-establish a dialectic, which is proper to all democratic societies, entailing both confrontation and coexistence. But Chávez attempts to prevent this at all costs, evident in his insistence on maintaining a climate of pugnacity. The opposition has to be clearly orientated, not just to "knock down" Chávez but also to win the elections in 2006, beginning with the parliamentary elections in 2005. Let us hope that by then the depressing effects of the RR will have been overcome and that we will be able to tackle those elections with more positive policies, rather than, as has been the case until now, the attitude of being "dispossessed", which was adopted during the regional elections. The opposition have to understand that they are fighting from a rearguard position. At the moment, Chávez is now very comfortable. Having been nationally legitimized (at least by half of the country) and also internationally recognized, he allows himself mad fits of personal openness and expansiveness, although staying true to himself, he adorns such occasions with his "crude speech" (or, as it is described by López Maya Dixit, *"discurso ramplón"*) and a constant torrent of insults against his adversaries, in which he considers anyone who opposes him to be a "fascist" or an "oligarch". All this has produced devastating effects, given that the CD have behaved erratically and fell into the trap of denouncing a fraud (not to mention *Fedecámaras*[34] and the *Confederación de Trabajadores de Venezuela* [Confederation of Workers of Venezuela]), both of which are visibly disorientated). The CD has responded to Chávez with high-sounding but hollow and unfocused declarations, which have only ended up causing them to become politically isolated. A fight from the rear is what today impels the defence of all remaining democratic space, as precarious as it may be, against an authoritarian tendency that could be formidably boosted by the results of the regional and local elections.

Before anything else, policy demands an accurate understanding of the nature of the government. A great many of the mistakes made at different times by the opposition—which have been driven either by the effective powers within the country (the media, economy and the military) or by other political parties and civilian organizations—have partly resulted from an erroneous diagnosis of the character of *Chávismo*. Having defined Chávez's government as a "totalitarian dictatorship", the strategy adopted by the opposition was rebellious, with the tendency to "knee-jerk" reactions, which has led to expensive defeats. Although there is a strong authoritarian tendency in the Chávez cult, accentuated by the autocratic temperament of its leader, this does not allow us at the moment to define the current regime either as a dictatorship or as totalitarian. The margins of democracy and legality in the country have not yet disappeared, and the formal characteristics of democratic life still survive, as badly shaken as they may be; but this does not mean that they are not in permanent danger of being even further emaciated by *Chávismo*. We still have a significant margin for political action. Concerning their potential to summon the masses and take action, the forces that oppose the regime today are a lot stronger than they were in 1999. The mass of opposition is immense and has demonstrated a capacity for being combative. Up until 2000, the size of its electoral base was known. Now we know that it is not only large but that it has the capacity to mobilize the population. In the three most important cities in the country the Chávez cult is in a minority, and wherever they won in urban Venezuela it was in a ratio of 60:40, or in the worst case 70:30. This reveals that there are already many people who are no longer under the spell of the charismatic leader. (On the other hand, in the places where Chávez lost, the ratios were generally between 90:10 and 80:20). If we consider that the large majority of the population were against Chávez, and that, in addition, there were others, who, being uncertain of the immediate future, voted for him, even though they were opposed to him, then we should not abandon

---

[34] The *Federación de Cámaras y Asociaciones de Comercio y Producción de Venezuela* (Venezuelan Federation of Chambers of Commerce) oversees twelve trade organizations: banking, agriculture, commerce, construction, energy, manufacturing, media, mining, ranching, insurance, transportation, and tourism.

ourselves to pessimism and discouragement, not to mention resignation. From this perspective of formidable support, a victorious force can be built, a force able to accommodate, within a unified political framework, the aspirations for a better life and the profound desire for justice and equality that resides in the poor and the socially excluded, many of whom still undoubtedly recognize themselves in, and identify themselves with the cult of Chávez. This force is like the undying passion for freedom and democracy that is a natural right of the entire nation, and which is the only thing that can provide a firm grounding for a just society, precisely because it is only by being democratic that a society becomes just.

(I am writing right before the regional elections, the results of which could be catastrophic for the opposition, should the strong tendency to abstain persist, in which case negative developments would become accentuated in the current situation. But this only means that we will have to be patient and tenacious, and that work at ground level is imperative).

Caracas, September 2004